BEN ASHER'S CREED

A Study of the History of the Controversy

THE SOCIETY OF BIBLICAL LITERATURE
MASORETIC STUDIES

edited by
Harry M. Orlinsky

Number 3
BEN ASHER'S CREED
A Study of the History of the Controversy

by
Aron Dotan

SCHOLARS PRESS
Missoula, Montana

BEN ASHER'S CREED
A Study of the History of the Controversy

by
Aron Dotan

Published by
SCHOLARS PRESS
for
The Society of Biblical Literature
and
The International Organization for Masoretic Studies

Distributed by

SCHOLARS PRESS
University of Montana
Missoula, Montana 59812

BEN ASHER'S CREED
A Study of the History of the Controversy

by

Aron Dotan

Library of Congress Cataloging in Publication Data
Dotan, Aron, 1928-
    Ben Asher's creed.

    (Masoretic studies ; no. 3)
    "A first version of this study was published . . . in
1957 in the Hebrew journal Sinai."
    Bibliography: p.
    1. Aaron ben Moses ben Asher. 2. Karaites.
I. Title. II. Series.
BM755.A12D67   296.8'1   76-27649
ISBN 0-89130-084-8

                Printed in the United States of America

                    Printing Department
                    University of Montana
                    Missoula, Montana 59812

TO RUTH

TABLE OF CONTENTS

8

PREFACE

A first version of this study was published back in 1957 in the Hebrew journal *Sinai*. It seems that it may not have come to the attention of the wide scholarly public interested in Biblical and masoretic studies, especially outside Israel, consequently the views expressed regarding Ben Asher's creed remained to a great extent unknown. We feel therefore that a renewed attempt to present these views, especially before those who are not well read in modern Hebrew, is now in place. In this new presentation, consideration has been given to the development of research in this field during the years that have elapsed, and to the new opinions expressed in this matter. This is therefore meant to be not only an English formulation of the hypothesis put forward years ago, but also an updated account of the whole problem in which our previous attitude and ideas have been re-examined and consequently, some details, to an extent, remolded.

I extend my gratitude to friends and colleagues, who by kind cooperation and encouragement made this publication possible, among others:

Professor Sid Z. Leiman suggested the whole idea of presenting this study to the English reading public and also made some valuable remarks,

Professor Harry M. Orlinsky, the Editor of the present series, was warmly encouraging and friendly cooperative,

Mr. Bernard Scharfstein and KTAV Publishing House contributed towards the publication.

10

Thanks are also due to the Society of Biblical Literature for the publishing of this study, to Tel-Aviv University for its aid in the publication, to Professor Raphael Posner, who translated the original Hebrew and made some useful suggestions, and to Mrs. Daniela Korem, who typed the final camera-ready manuscript.

Aron Dotan

Tel-Aviv University

May 1976

INTRODUCTION

The vexing question of Ben Asher's religious belief has occupied the attention of scholars for many years. Since the 1860's, at which time it was first suggested that Ben Asher was a Karaite, there has been bitter controversy on the subject which has at times been accompanied by accusations of heresy and Karaite zeal. This is not surprising in view of the fact that the problem is a delicate one in which the historical aspect has often been subordinate to the theological.

Ben Asher has been considered the authority in all matters of the traditional text of the Bible, particularly with regard to vocalization, accentuation, *plene* and deficient spellings, open and closed sections (*parashiyyot*) etc. While it is true that at the beginning there were others who also devoted themselves to these subjects, as the lists recording the differences between him and Ben Naftali clearly show, from the time, however, that Maimonides accepted Ben Asher's version, he has become the final authority in this field.

Thus, when the claim was made that Ben Asher was a Karaite, one of the most important foundations of the text of the Bible as we have it was disturbed. Behind all the discussions on the subject lurked the question: Is it really possible that the text of the Bible that has been accepted by Rabbanite Jewry for so many generations is based on the version of a heretic? For those who refused to accept this thesis the most important evidence was the fact that Maimonides accepted Ben Asher's version, which he surely would not have done had Ben Asher been a Karaite; the opposition view justified Maimonides by saying that he had not been aware of Ben Asher's beliefs and that indeed a surprising "accident" had occured.

The great controversy about Ben Asher continued to the end of the last century and finally subsided for want of any new real evidence. However the problem was not resolved. Each side established its own proofs but did not always succeed in completely invalidating the proofs offered by the opposite side. In any event the new suggestion was not really accepted by most of the writers on the subject.

However, when Klar succeeded in reading the name, Ben Asher, in the superscription of a manuscript of Saadia Gaon's *Essa Meshali* the whole question of Ben Asher's religious faith took a new turn. Klar re-examined the old arguments in the light of his discovery, reestablished their validity and thus completed a picture of Ben Asher. Klar claimed, categorically, that Ben Asher was a Karaite; a claim that became generally accepted in learned circles and against which no objections were raised for a long time.

In discussing the problem anew, it is impossible to ignore its historical development, particularly since no problem existed until the controversy started, and it was the controversy itself that aggravated the problem. It is, therefore, only correct that we examine critically the old arguments individually before presenting our own view.

1. THE PROOFS THAT BEN ASHER WAS A KARAITE

In order to facilitate an easier understanding of the development of the problem we shall separate the proofs and classify them into three main headings although in the actual controversy they were interwoven and interconnected.

The first category consists of those proofs brought from literary sources close to Ben Asher chronologically; the second category is those proofs brought from his treatise *Diqduqé Ha-Teᶜamim* (=DQHT); and the third is the proofs deduced from the colophons of manuscripts attributed to Ben Asher.

1.1. Proofs from Grammatical and other Literary Sources

The first to broach the question was S. Pinsker who, in 1860, wrote:[1] "I am not afraid to state that, in my opinion, *all* the masoretes, grammarians, vocalizers and accentuators (*including Ben Asher and Ben Naftali*) who devoted themselves exclusively to those tasks and of whom there is no indication elsewhere that they ever studied Talmud, *are to be suspected* of Karaism; even if they were not overt Karaites they are still to be suspected of such tendencies and sympathies ... This is also my opinion with regard to those scholars who devoted themselves to compiling lexicons and explaining the Bible in a literal manner.   However, these suspicions only apply to such scholars from the time of Anan till about fifty years after Saadia Gaon; after

that time Rabbanites also did that work,although there is no indication
that they did anything else."[2]

Schorr[3] already objected to the arbitrary judgement contained in
the above statement, for it is surely impossible to suspect of Karaism
everybody for whom there is no proof that he was a Rabbanite; but Graetz
offered evidence for Pinsker's axiomatic assumption. He accepted the
opinion that Ben Asher was a Karaite and discovered several facts on
which to base it. We will deal here only with the four that belong to
the "literary" category.[4]

1.1.0.1.   Ben Asher is often given the appellation המלמד (lit. the
teacher); thus in MSL:[5] המלמד אהרן בן משה בן אשר נוחו בגן עדן, and also
in other manuscripts. This title is used only among Karaites.

1.1.0.2.   Dunash ben Labrat records[6] that Saadia Gaon wrote responsa
against (i.e. objected to) a certain Ben Asher, something which he did
only against Karaites and other heretics. Furthermore, Saadia did not
address Ben Asher with respect in his responsum[7] from which it follows
that the Ben Asher must have been a Karaite. Since Saadia addresses
his respondent, Ben Asher, in the second person (תֵּלַף) the responsum must
have been written to a contemporary, i.e., to Aaron Ben Asher.[8]

1.1.0.3.   Dunash and his pupil, Yehudi ben Sheshet, do not mention
Ben Asher in their objections to Menahem and his disciples; this can be
explained by the fact that Dunash was a Palestinian (in Graetz's
opinion) and, as a younger contemporary of Ben Asher, knew that the
latter was a Karaite.[9]

1.1.0.4.   The Karaite, Judah Hadassi speaks of Ben Asher as belonging
to his faith since he mentions him with the eulogistic formula

רוח די תניחנו (May the spirit of God grant him rest).[10]

We will now weigh these arguments individually:

1.1.1.   It has already been argued[11] that even among the Rabbanites
there were מלמדים i.e. school teachers whose occupation was
such; it appears that the first masoretes and grammarians were such
teachers who supported themselves by instructing children in Bible and
reading.[12]

As far as Ben Asher is concerned it must be pointed out that in
most of the places where he is mentioned with the appellation מלמד the
term seems to have a technical meaning. Thus in MSL[13] and in MSA[14]
(ראש המלמדים, המלמד הגדול)[15] as well as at the beginning of Mishael ben
Uzziel's list of variations[16] (אלכ׳לף אלד׳י אכ׳תלף פיה אלמעלמין: the
variations on which the two teachers, מעלמין,differed)[17] and in the
Treatise on the Shewa[18] ("..... there were also, together with the above
mentioned elders, who were great מלמדים, other מלמדים and they were
great sages in Bible reading and competent in all matters of vocalization,
accentuation, Masora and their use.")[19] In all these sources - particularly the last two - the technical use of the term, מלמד, is clear,
i.e. teacher, a profession which was never exclusive to the Karaites.

As is well known, the teacher and the scribe performed identical
functions. However, it is worthwhile establishing this fact with regard
to the period under discussion.[20] Saadia Gaon refers to a woman who
asked the teacher (אלמעלם) to release her son with the words:
יא ספרא אפני ברי[21] calling the מעלם a ספרא; this is realiable evidence
since Saadia tells the story with regard to a completely different point.
Graetz himself in a footnote to this argument[22] cites a manuscript in
which the opinion of המורה יעקב בן נפתלי הסופר is quoted. In the

colophon of MSA Ben Asher is described as אדון הסופרים ... וראש המלמדים

and elsewhere as   המלמד הגדול ר' אהרן בן משה בן אשר ... הוא אמן גדול

בתקון הסופרים[23]; the term אמן as used here certainly means "scribe"

just as האומנים הראשונים[24] are הסופרים הראשונים.[25]

Furthermore, the work of the teacher/scribe by its very nature
could not have been exclusive to the Karaites and indeed one finds this
appellation attached to sages of whose orthodoxy there can be no doubt:
מרנא ורבי אפרים ... ברבי שמריה המלמד[26] ...; ... בן מלמדי ... מרנא ורבנא
עובדיהו הכהן המלמד[27]... and many others. A letter from the heads of the
Jerusalem Yeshiva to the Palestinian congregations is addressed, among
the other communal leaders, to the מלמדים.[28] These are only some
examples. The argument based on the use of the term, מלמד, is therefore
without foundation.

1.1.2.   No proof can be deduced from the fact (as it seemed to
          Graetz) that Saadia addressed Ben Asher in a disrespectful
manner since the three words, quoted by Dunash, have been otherwise
interpreted[29] in a way which implies no disrespect. However, Graetz's
point that Saadia only wrote objections against Karaites and other
heretics, from which it would follow that the Ben Asher addressed was a
Karaite, is valid notwithstanding Bacher's[30] refusal to accept it as
sufficient to establish that Ben Asher was a Karaite. We will return
to this point below (3.0.).

1.1.3.   Graetz's third argument is entirely unacceptable. The fact
          that Dunash and his pupil do not mention Ben Asher proves
nothing. Menahem, who was not a Palestinian and could be expected to be
ignorant of Ben Asher's alleged Karaism, also does not mention him, as
indeed Ben Asher's younger contemporary, David ben Abraham, who was a
Karaite and a Palestinian,[31] does not. Moreover, Dunash was not a

Palestinian. The silence about Ben Asher cannot prove anything about his religious affiliations; it only suggests that in his own generation - and in the 10th century generally - Ben Asher had not yet achieved the great fame which was later to be his.[32]

1.1.4. This argument has already been refuted.[33] The Karaites make no distinction between their own fellow sectarians and Rabbanites in the eulogistic formulas they apply where virulent controversy does not spoil relations. Thus Hadassi refers to יהודה בן דוד חיוג הספרדי ז"ל and נ"ע[34] יונה בן גנח. In the Karaite prayer book in the list of leading Karaite personalities three Rabbanite sages are mentioned accompanied by the formula זכרונם לברכה ולתחיה and are described as "the three pious men who will inherit paradise". In many sources which do not relate directly to the controversy with the Rabbanites, the latter are often referred to as "our bretheren".[35] Furthermore, the formula, רוח ה' תניחנו, is an ancient one which Yemenite and Babylonian Jews used and which is even found attached to Saadia himself.[36] In any event this "proof" for Ben Asher's Karaism is also without foundation.

Thus of the four proofs cited from literary sources, only the second has not yet been entirely refuted.

1.2. Proofs from *Diqduqé Ha-Ṭeʿamim*

Graetz[37] argues:

1.2.0.1. From the statement in DQHT (§3):
סדר הנביאים האשמרת התיכונה,שֶׁלּוֹם התורה כמעמד התורה, ומורים מהם הוריה כתורה[38] it is clear that Ben Asher considered the Prophets and the Hagiographa to be a part of the Pentateuch and complementary to it,

which opinion is held by the Karaites. Fürst[39] elaborated this claim
and contrasted the views of the Rabbanites and the Karaites on this
point: The former derive law (*halakha*) from the Pentateuch and the rest
of the Bible is seen only as קבלה (tradition) or "support" (for laws
otherwise derived); and ילפינן לא קבלה מדברי תורה דברי [40] ("Words of Tora
cannot be derived from words of קבלה.") The latter, however, derive
halakha from the whole Bible and consider the whole Bible to be תורה.
Ben Asher agrees with the Karaite view that the Prophets and the
Hagiographa are התורה שלום (complementary to the תורה) or אשלמתא[41] and
כתורה הוריה מהם מורים (one derives law from them as from the תורה).

1.2.0.2.   The main halakhic hermeneutic principles of the Karaites
are generally considered to be three: כתוב, the biblical text; היקש,
analogy; and קיבוץ, consensus of opinion (alternatively called עדה or
הסכמה[42]) and all are of equal authority for deriving the law. Ben Asher
(§3) mentions one of these principles, המוקש (the analogy), and even
states that the law resulting from its use is to be regarded as though
it were explicitly written in the text.[43]

1.2.0.3.   Ben Asher's statement (§9):

על שלשה דרכים אמורה. רָבָּם בדעה קשורה ... ומהם בצווי אסורה ומהם בעדה
עצורה indicates a complete acceptance of the Karaite hermeneutic
principles: דעה is the analogy (היקש or ידיעה "the knowledge") and עדה
(another ms. כנסת) is the consensus (קיבוץ, הסכמה).[44]

1.2.0.4.   The term משכיל is occasionally used about Ben Asher: e.g.
המשכילים והמזהירים יזהירו כזהר הרקיע בגן עדן.[45] In one place he
actually uses the term himself: והמשכילים יבינו.[46] This appellation
exclusively used by the Karaites.
    We will now examine these arguments.

1.2.1.   The terms שילום and אשלמתא fit the Rabbanite point of view
better than they do the Karaite, for it is particularly the
former who see the Prophets and the Hagiographa as well as the Oral Law
as a complement to the Pentateuch. The Karaites consider the Prophets
and the Hagiographa not as a complement to *Torah* but rather as *Torah*
itself. The expression שילום התורה, as interpreted by Graetz, is
therefore a proof to the contrary.

Furthermore, in DQHT the term שילום is applied to the Prophetic
Books of the Bible only and not to the Hagiographa which is not described
as being כמעמד התורה (equal in authority to the Pentateuch). Such a
distinction between the Prophets and the Hagiographa is foreign to Karaite
theology.[47]

It should also be pointed out that שילום and אשלמתא do not seem to
mean "complement" but rather "transmission"[48] which is the sense of the
verb שלם as used in Midrash and *piyyut*[49] and also in cognate languages
(Syriac: משלמנותא = tradition,like Hebrew מסורת). The terms שילום and
אשלמתא are therefore close to the term קבלה which is how the Prophetic
Books are sometimes called in the Talmud (דברי קבלה); in a later period
these books are also called אשלמתא because the alternative term, מסורה or
מסורת, was already being used for another purpose.

Saphir[50] has pointed out that the phrase[51] ולמדים ממנו הורייה כתורה
means that law may be derived from the Prophets only and not from the
Hagiographa.[52] Furthermore, the talmudic dictum,דברי תורה מדברי קבלה לא,
ילפינן means that one cannot apply the principle of גזרה שוה (analogy)
from the text of the Prophets[53] to that of the Pentateuch since the
language (on which the principle of גזרה שוה[analogy]is based) of each is
unique, but one may derive law (דין תורה) from the Prophets.[54] This is
the thrust of the use of the words ד ב ר י תורה ...לא ילפינן rather than
ד י ן תורה ...לא ילפינן.[55] Oppenheim cites several examples of this[56]
e.g. דבר זה מתורת משה לא למדנו עד שבא יחזקאל ולימדנו (T.B. Yevamot 22b.,

83b.) and דברי קבלה כדברי תורה דמו (T.B. Rosh Ha-Shana 19a.) which is an
exact parallel of the phrase שלום התורה כמעמד התורה. Oppenheim also
deduces from the phrase ומורים בה הוריה[57] that one may derive הוריה
(teaching) from the Prophets but not actual מצוות (commandments), which
is in absolute opposition to the beliefs of the Karaites who derive their
commandments from the whole Bible.

A further proof is that, in contradiction to the Karaites who
believe the whole Bible to be of equal authority and all actual *Torah*,
the author of DQHT calls the Hagiographa (§3) קבלה של אמת ("true
tradition").

1.2.1.1. However, since this refutation of Graetz's argument was
written, Wieder[58] has demonstrated that even the Karaites recognised the
primacy of the Pentateuch as a law source at least insofar as the number
of commandments is concerned. Thus the entire basis of Graetz's argument
is removed.

Wieder, however, has put forward a new argument. He claims that the
use of the word מקדש as a metaphor for the Bible is Karaite which the
Rabbanites, at the beginning, did not recognize. I hope to treat this
new argument elsewhere.

1.2.2. Analogy, as a hermeneutic principle, exists in Rabbanite
methodology and certainly cannot be considered to be an
indication of Karaism.[59] Fürst was apparently aware that analogy in
itself is no such indication unless it is accompanied by the other
Karaite hermeneutic principles, and he therefore attempted to discover
all three Karaite principles in the phrase of DQHT: להודיע שכל הכתוב
והבטוי והמוקש. To this end he artificially explained[60] the term בטוי as
Mittheilung i.e. the hermeneutic principle of transmission (העתקה)!

The scholars even differ with regard to the exact text that should be taken as the basis for this argument or its refutation. Graetz and his followers relied on the text as it appears in the *Quntres Ha-Masoret*[61] while the opposing camp, Saphir, Oppenheim and others, relied on MSC.[62] Since MSC is undoubtedly the older of the two and was copied by Moses Ben Asher and since it does not have the word המוקש, it would follow, according to the opposing view, that the *Quntres Ha-Masoret* version is later and corrupt and thus unreliable. Furthermore, since, in their opinion, Moses Ben Asher was a Rabbanite it is inconceivable that his son, Aaron, could have been a Karaite.

In order to clarify this point we here present the end of the passage in question, as it appears in the two versions, in order to explain the relationship between them.

Quntres Ha-Masoret	MSC
...להודיע	...וכל זה להודיע
	לכל באי העולם
	כבוד קדושתם וגודל שבחם ועוצם תפארתם
שכל הכתוב והבטוי והמוקש לכתב הקדש	שכל הברוי וכל[63]העליונות והתחתונות
והנקוד והטעמים ואותיות תלויים	5 והעתידות והקדמניות והחדשות
ואותיות קטנים וגדולים ועקומים והנקודות	
5 והחצונים וסתומות[64]ופתוחים ונכתב ולא	
נקרא ונקרא ולא נכתב ואותיות מנוזרות	
שהן על סידורן ועל חלקם ועל גבולם ועל סדורם	כי הם על חלקם ועל גבולם ועל סדורם
ועל שנונם	וכן העליונים והתחתונים
אם רבו בשמות ובמנין[65]	אם רבו בשמות ובמיניהם
10 הם שבים לסדר הזה	הם שבים לסידור הזה
בבית קדש הקדשים והקדש וחצר אהל מועד	10 בבית קדש הקדשים וחצר אהל מועד

The section as it appears in MSC discusses the relationship of the Cosmos to the Bible. The upper and lower worlds, the past and the future are all in the Bible and are based on it. The Bible has three (descending) levels of holiness (or importance), Torah, Prophets and Hagiographa which are parallel to the Holy of Holies (of the Temple), the holy section (of the Temple) and the courtyard of the Tent of Meeting.[66] This is approximately the general meaning of the passage and although some of the details are obscure and some seem to be corrupted,[67] the passage is still unified and coherent. An indication of the coherence is the tripartite motif which runs through the entire description of the Creation: in the spatial description הברוי, העליונות, התחתונות -- man (the most important of the created for whose sake all else was created), the upper world and the lower world; in the chronological description העתידות, הקדמניות, החדשות -- future, past and present.[68] The tripartite division of the Bible, on which all these rest, thus becomes perfectly understandable. The other expressions in the passage, which are not connected with the above theme, still have this "three" pattern:

כבוד קדושתם, גודל שבחם, עוצם תפארתם; על סידורן, על חלקם, על גבולם.[69]

The passage as it is in the *Quntres Ha-Masoret*, however, is incoherent. The universal theme, which treats the relationship of the Creation to the Bible and which is thus addressed to "all creatures", is missing, and in its place there are textual instructions for the reader and the student which are completely unconnected to both the preceeding section,[70] the tripartite division of the Bible, and the following section, the various levels of holiness which itself relates to the divisions of the Bible as explained above. It is therefore reasonable to assume that the new section (lines 2 - 6) was inserted in order to give the entire section more of a "Masoretic" flavor. So far regarding the textual relationship of the two versions as far as the present discussion is concerned.[71]

Without entering into an explanation of the first line of the
insertion as it is in the *Quntres Ha-Masoret* (line 2), it is worthwhile
to examine exactly what is listed in this insertion. Four subjects are
mentioned: 1) Additions to the body of the biblical text (vocalization,
accentuation, dotted letters and separated [מנוזרות] letters);
2) Additions outside the actual body of the text (חיצונים;[72] "written
but not read" and "read but not written" instructions); 3) Peculiarities
in the writing of letters (suspended letters, small, large and crooked
letters[73]); and 4) The arrangement of the lines (closed and open
sections).

The most important item, which is missing from this inventory, is
the actual consonantal text, and this is certainly meant by the words,
הכתוב והבטוי in the first sentence. These two words are an exact
parallel of the talmudic methods of interpretation, יש אם למסורת ("the
consonantal text is authoritative") and יש אם למקרא ("the text as
pronounced is authoritative"). הכתוב, or as in other mss. הכתב, means the
מסורת, i.e., the written signs, the letters, and הבטוי means the text as
it is traditionally pronounced. These two methods of interpretation are
Rabbanite.[74]

In this context, between the הכתוב והבטוי and the various additions
to the consonantal text, it is impossible to interpret the words מוקש
לכתב הקדש as being the principle of analogy of the Karaites. Even Graetz
realized that his interpretation did not fit the text and so emended it
to read והמוקש דומה לכתב הקודש,[75] a completely arbitrary emendation for
which no justification can be found in any of the mss. or printed
versions -- neither those of which Graetz was aware nor those that have
since been discovered.[76] We can only understand these two words as a
sort of heading for all the other items listed; perhaps as Baer
understood it: "Tied and connected to the holy text,"[77] i.e., all the
various technical aids for the application of the two methods of

interpretation.

We must still investigate the closing sentence:
הם שבים לסדר הזה בבית קדש הקדשים וחצר אהל מועד. The fact that in the
Quntres Ha-Masoret and sister versions the word והקדש is missing[78] is
evidence that we have here a continuation of the "correcting" of the
entire passage, and that the deletion was deliberate in order to
establish the whole new version. Once the universal content had been
removed and replaced by the Masoretical-grammatical there is obviously
no place for the three levels of holiness but rather for only two, הכתב
והבטוי, which are the consonantal text -- the Holy of Holies — and
everything added to that text -- the courtyard of the Tent of Meeting.

In any event it is clear that Graetz's argument with regard to the
hermeneutic principle of analogy is untenable.

1.2.3.   No refutation has yet been offered against Graetz's third proof
from DQHT and it deserves a close examination. It is true that
the terms דעה and עדה are used by the Karaites as names for hermeneutic
principles[79] but nevertheless the terms as used in DQHT cannot be taken
out of their context and interpreted independently. In order to
demonstrate that the author of DQHT was listing Karaite principles, which
are at least three in number, Graetz would have to find the third; but
the word צווי is not open to such an interpretation - even if we ignore
the variant ms. reading of כנסת in place of עדה - no such name exists in
any Karaite source for a hermeneutic principle. As long as he cannot
succeed in explaining this word his argument is untenable.[80]

Klar attempted to fill this deficiency and explained צווי as מצוה,
which would mean the literal meaning of the text,[81] and thus arrived at
three principles in this sentence: דעה, צווי (= the text) and עדה (=קיבוץ,
הסכמה consensus). But for the Karaites the principle of analogy is the
most typical and indeed they are known by the name אלקיאסין (i.e.,

masters of the analogy).[82] How is it possible that this important and typical principle should be missing here?[83] It would appear that Graetz was sensitive to this problem and because of it was not specific in his interpretation of the word דעה[84] and left it as analogy *or* knowledge.[85] He thus, without committing himself, led the reader to interpret the word as referring to the principle of analogy. However, besides the semantic difficulty, how is it possible that the author of DQHT would call this important principle by two different names: דעה here and מוקש elsewhere (see above 1.2.0.2) which is, according to Graetz, also the analogy? We are, after all, not dealing here with flowery descriptive writing but rather with fixed terms which refer to matters of principle. It must also be borne in mind that the term דעה serves a different purpose in the same inventory of values. It is thus impossible to interpret דעה as meaning the principle of analogy.

As stated, Klar interpreted דעה literally and according to him we have here the hermeneutic principles: כתוב, דעה, and קיבוץ. Is it, however, conceivable that the author of DQHT would list three principles and not that of analogy which he does, according to Graetz whose opinion Klar accepts, mention elsewhere? If he accepts four principles then why does he not list them here where he is, according to this view, reviewing them briefly? How can he state that three ways are ordained (על שלשה דרכים אמורה) when he believes that there are actually four ways?[86]

Furthermore, if by the use of the word דעה our author meant the Karaite principle of "(individual) opinion" how could he state that "most of them (the commandments) are bound up with דעה" (רובם בדעה קשורה)? Most commandments are not based on דעה; certainly no more than they are on the main hermeneutic source, the actual text! To the contrary, many, if not most, Karaite sages of that period did not accept the principle of דעה at all.[87] It is also incorrect to state that commandments arrived at by way of דעה "will never change as long as the heavens exist"

(לא ישתנו עד בלתי שמי שפרה); the very nature of the principle of דעה allows each sage to rely on his own o p i n i o n and derive laws at his own discretion. Therefore not only is it incorrect to make the above statement with regard to Karaite law generally, but even an individual Karaite is permitted to change his own mind and change or cancel a law which he had previously derived by his own דעה, and which he observed until he changed his mind.[88]

Finally, in addition to everything stated above, the interpretation of צווי as the actual text is incorrect. This interpretation[89] is based on the word מצוה as found in the writings of Nissi ben Noah from which we will present the relevant passage:[90]

"The knowledge of תורה and the performance of its commandments can be divided into two parts. The first is the commandment which Almighty God commanded in the תורה to do and observe which is clear and revealed   (א' מהם מצוה שצוה אל שדי בתורה

לעשותה ולשמרה והיא ברורה וגלויה) such as 'Observe the Sabbath day to keep it holy' (Deut. 5:12) and 'Honor thy father and mother' (Deut. 5:15) and such like .... The second is the hidden (צפונה)[91] and concealed commandment which can be divided into two categories. The first comprises the commandments in which only a part is explicit, the rest being derived by use of the analogy such as Almighty God having commanded 'Thou shalt not plough with an ox and ass together' (Deut. 22:10) to which, by analogy, we add the fatling and the mule; and such as 'and there fell there an ox or an ass' (Ex. 21:33) which includes a sheep and a horse because 'ox' includes all clean animals and 'ass' includes all unclean animals by analogy. The second category is those commandments which are not clear and revealed and are not explained in the *Tora* and for which there is

nothing else to make an analogy to and thus explain them. We
only know them through the oral transmission of father to son,
former to latter ...."

The interpretation of מצוה as the literal meaning of the text is
based on the use of the word at the beginning of the passage: מצוה שצוה
אל שדי בתורה ... והיא ברורה וגלויה However even the most cursory
examination of this sentence shows that the principle of the literal
text (הכתוב) is meant by the words והיא ברורה וגלויה, meaning
commandments clear and revealed in the text as opposed to those
commandments which are hidden and concealed, i.e., which are not explicit
in the text and which must be arrived at by the other hermeneutic
principles. That the word מצוה does not refer to any principle is clear
also from the fact that it is used with regard to the other categories
as well; both with regard to the "hidden and concealed commandment"
(מצוה צפונה וסתורה) i.e. not appearing in the literal text, as well as
with regard to its two types: "the commandments in which only a part is
explicit, the rest to be derived by a n a l o g y"   (מצות שזכר ואמר
מעט מהרבה לחייבנו להקיש כמותם) and "the commandments which are not clear
and revealed .... which we know only through the o r a l   transmission
of father to son"   (מצות דברים שאינם ברורים וגלוים ... אלא בהגדת אב לבן).
The word מצוה cannot be explained otherwise than by its normal meaning
"commandment" and cannot therefore serve as a source to interpret the
צווי mentioned in the DQHT as meaning the principle of כתוב.

1.2.3.1.   We have demonstrated that the attempt to discover the
Karaite hermeneutic principles in the DQHT was unsuccessful. We will
attempt here to explain the sentence in question in another manner. In
order to do so we present it within its context (§9):

תחלה הנחיל אל דברות עשרה, ועוד משפט ואזהרה, וגם קלה וחמורה, בַּאֵר הֵיטֵב
מְבֹאָרָה, על שלשה דרכים אמורה, רֻבָּם בדעה קשורה, ויפה ברורה, ומהם בְּצִוּוּי

אסורה, ומהם בְּעֵדָה (or בכנסת) עצורה, לא ישתנו עד בלתי שְׁמֵי שָׁפְרָה

The approximate explanation is: In addition to the Ten Commandments were
added mandatory commandments (משפט) and prohibitions (אזהרה)[92], light
and severe,[93] amply explained and stated in three ways: Most are
dependent on knowledge and intelligence and are easily understandable;
some are dependent on a scriptural command (cannot be understood by
intelligence) and others kept and preserved in the Congregation of
Israel (עדת ישראל or כנסת ישראל) and they are the commandments of the
Oral Law.[94] These commandments will never change.

The sentence in question fits very nicely the accepted division of
the commandments of the Torah into rational commandments dependent on
the intelligence (דעה)[95] and arbitrary commandments (צווי)[96] to which
are to be added scribal (or Rabbinic) commandments (מדברי סופרים) which
are "kept in the congregation".

1.2.4.   Even if we ignore the fact that the word משכיל, as it is cited
          by Graetz, occurs within the context of a biblical quotation,[97]
the term used independently was acceptable to the Rabbanites and the
fact that the Karaites adopted it never prevented the Rabbanites from
using it. Many have cited proofs of this from the usage of various
periods,[98] and perhaps a decisive proof[99] is to be found in the writings
of a Karaite contemporary of Aaron Ben Asher's: Qirqisānī testifies
explicitly that the Rabbanites claimed that they, the Rabbanites, were
the משכילים and the מורים.[100] The expression is even found in Saadia
Gaon's *Essa Meshali*[101] (מצדיקי ומשכילַי ומזהירַי) and the anonymous
Rabbanite author of the *Ancient Questions in the Bible* describes the
seven sages who stood at the head of the *Yeshiva* as   שבעת החברים
משכילי דברים עתיקים.[102] It therefore seems that the term משכילים was used
by both Rabbanites and Karaites, and Mann has already pointed out that
this term as well as אבלי ציון was borrowed by the Karaites from the

Rabbanites.[103] The fact that the Karaites used משכילים to describe their sages may be explained by the fact that the term "Rabbis" (רבנים) had too much of a Rabbanite flavor.

1.2.5. The arguments brought from DQHT[104] for Ben Asher's Karaism are without foundation and before we treat the third category of proofs, a general note is in place. All the scholars involved in the controversy assumed that the then current edition of DQHT[105] was the work of Ben Asher and treated each word in it as though Ben Asher wrote it. This however has never been proved and those who published the book were careful to note the fact.[106] Even if it were conclusively proved that Ben Asher did write the relevant sections, scattered words and expressions cannot serve as evidence for his religious beliefs especially since the book does not deal with law or theology.

The actual language of the book is obscure even when its intent is clear and there can be no doubt that copyists corrupted the text when they did not understand it. It is, therefore, exceedingly difficult to establish the original text from amongst the corruptions and additions that have accumulated over the centuries. Even had we not been able to refute all the proofs tendered for Ben Asher's Karaism, insofar as they are based on the DQHT, they would still be unreliable as long as it has not been conclusively proven that the sections on which they rely were part of the original work.

Now that it is clear that of the two passages in question, one (§9) does not belong at all to DQHT and the other (§3) was certainly not written by Aaron Ben Asher,[107] there is no basis whatsoever for Graetz's arguments.

1.3.   Proofs from the Colophons

We will now deal with the proofs that Graetz brought from the colophons of the *Cairo Codex* (= MSC) and the *Aleppo Codex* (= MSA).

1.3.0.1.   The famous ms. of the Prophetic Books in the Karaite Synagogue in Cairo was written, according to one of the colophons at the end, by Moses Ben Asher, the father of Aaron. Graetz[108] first established that the father was a Karaite which strengthened his argument that the son was also a Karaite. The following are his arguments:

1.3.0.1.1.   It is clear from the sentence[109] כתבתי זה המחזור שלמקרא that it was part of a whole Bible. This copy was intended for public reading in the synagogue on "Sabbaths, New Moons and Festivals".[110] Since Rabbanites do not read from an entire Bible in the synagogue it follows that this copy was meant for the exclusive use of the Karaites.[111]

1.3.0.1.2.   The owner of the ms., Jabez ben Solomon, dedicated it not just to ordinary Karaites but to the exemplary Karaites "who fix the festivals by the sighting of the moon" (העושים את המועדות על ראית הירח)[112]. From this it follows that Jabez was an extreme Karaite and such a Karaite would certainly not order a Bible from a Rabbanite scribe. From this it would follow that Moses Ben Asher was a Karaite.

1.3.0.1.3.   A sentence in one of the colophons:
... עדת נביאים ... המבינים כל נסתרות ... לא כיחדו דבר ממה שניתן להם ולא הוסיפו מאמר על מה שנמסר להם ...[113] indicates the view, also expressed in §3 of DQHT, that the Prophets and the Hagiographa are complementary to the Pentateuch and that thus the Oral Law is superfluous.

1.3.0.2.   After it has been proven that Moses Ben Asher was a Karaite

it seems that his son, Aaron Ben Asher, also followed his father's
faith. However, as far as Aaron is concerned, Graetz added further
proofs relying on MSA which, according to the colophon at the end, Aaron
Ben Asher "pointed it and furnished it with Masora". Graetz's claims
here are:[114]

1.3.0.2.1. The ms. was handed over for safekeeping to the two
brothers, Josiahu and Jehezkiahu the sons of David the son of Boaz,
who were officials (נשיאים) of the Karaite community and descendants of
Anan.

1.3.0.2.2. The author of the colophon does permit Rabbanites to see
the ms. but only in order to check other scrolls against it and not for
public reading.

1.3.0.2.3. Israel of Basra who dedicated the manuscript was a Karaite
as is obvious from the colophon.

1.3.0.2.4. The note before the colophon at the beginning of the
manuscript "Sanctified for Rabbanite Israel ..." (קודש לה' על ישראל
הרבנים ...) is a later addition since, in the reader's Torah which was
copied from the manuscript in 1570 for Moses Isserlis of Cracow the note
does not appear. From this it follows that the note was added after
the end of the 16th century when the manuscript passed into Rabbanite
hands.

1.3.1. Graetz's arguments need detailed consideration.

1.3.1.1. If MSC was a section of an entire Bible, the scribe would
have written the colophon either at the beginning (i.e. before the
Pentateuch) or at the end (i.e. after the Hagiographa). It is very
unlikely that such a detailed colophon as ours would have been written

in the middle of a manuscript. From the fact that the colophon does
appear at the end of the Prophets it is clear that the manuscript did
not originally include the Hagiographa; whether it originally included
the Pentateuch is difficult to establish. An examination of photographs
of the manuscript does not indicate that it did include the Pentateuch
since the manuscript starts at the beginning of the Book of Joshua.[115]
Indeed, a comparison of the later colophons which were not written by
Moses Ben Asher and the original colophon of Moses Ben Asher seems to
indicate the contrary. The late colophons contain the phrase "This
codex of the eight prophets ..."[116]   (... זה הדפתר שמונה נביאים שהקדיש)
while Moses Ben Asher's has "This codex ..."[117] (... זה הדיפתר מה שזכה)
which might indicate that the דפתר[118] originally contained only the
Books of the Prophets. Furthermore it is unlikely that Jabez ben Solomon,
the owner of the manuscript, would have disassembled a complete manuscript
of Pentateuch and Prophets and dedicated to the Jerusalem Karaites only
the Prophets.[119]

The term מחזור is also no indication since it does not necessarily
mean a   c o m p l e t e   Bible manuscript but is used in the sense of
the Modern Hebrew מהדורה found in a similar sense in the Palestinian
Talmud in the form of מחזירה[120] and in the Babylonian Talmud as מהדורא[121]
When the intention was to a complete Bible the author of the colophon to
MSA used the phrase   מחזור   מ ק ר א   ש ל ם.
Even if MSC was originally a complete Bible which was meant to be
read publicly in Synagogue, it is still no proof that Moses Ben Asher
was a Karaite. Of the six colophons at the end of the manuscript, only
two are in the same script as the actual manuscript itself, while the
others, including the three in which the dedication of the manuscript to
the Jerusalem Karaites is mentioned, are in a different hand and inserted
with difficulty in the margins of the page. Graetz ignored this fact
completely[122] and assumed that all the colophons were equally authentic

and from the quill of Moses Ben Asher. Not only did Graetz ignore this
fact, he even put a new colophon together by taking words and parts of
sentences from four existing colophons. Thus he "quotes":[123]"I, Moses
Ben Asher, wrote this codex (מחזור) of Bible...[124] which Jabez ben
Solomon the Babylonian acquired...[125] which he dedicated to the Jerusalem
Karaites...[126] who fix the festivals by the sighting of the moon so that
they should all read from it on Sabbaths, New Moons and festivals."[127]

From our analysis it seems that what happened was as follows: Moses
Ben Asher wrote the copy of the Prophetic Books and Jabez ben Solomon
b o u g h t[128] it from him. Jabez dedicated the manuscript to the
Karaites in Jerusalem although it is probable that Jabez retained it
during his lifetime[129] and the gift took effect only at his death. It is
possible that Jabez had been a Rabbanite at the time of the purchase and
later changed his affiliations, or that he bought the manuscript through
a third party who did not reveal the religious beliefs of the purchaser
to the scribe. This seems likely since Moses Ben Asher lived in
Tiberias and Jabez in Jerusalem or in Babylonia.[130] It is also possible
that Moses Ben Asher sold the manuscript to Jabez, fully aware of the fact
that the purchaser was a Karaite as happened in not a few cases.[131]
Whichever way it was, there is no connection with the religious
affiliations of Moses Ben Asher. According to his own testimony he wrote
the codex for study (להגות בו) and not for public reading in the
synagogue and therefore it was pointed and furnished with Masora. The
statement that the pointed manuscript was meant for synagogue reading
was not Ben Asher's but was made by the Karaite who dedicated it.

1.3.1.2.   With the above we have answered Graetz's second claim as
well.

1.3.1.3.   In order to clarify Graetz's third argument we here present the text of Moses Ben Asher's colophon on which it was based:[132]

אני משה בן אשר כתבתי זה המחזור שלמקרא על פי[133] כיד אלהי הטובה עלי
באר היטב במדינת מעזיה טבריה העיר ההוללה כשהבינו[134] עדת נביאים בחורי ד'
קדושי אלהינו המבינים כל נסתרות והמשפירים סוד חכמה אילי הצדק אנשי אמנה
לא כיחדו דבר ממה שניתן להם ולא הוסיפו מאמר על מה שנימסר להם והעצימו
והגדילו המק' עשרים וארבעה ספרים וייסדום באמונתם בטעמי שכל בפירוש דיבור
בחיך מתוק ביופי מאמר ...

(I, Moses Ben Asher have written this Codex of the Scripture according
to my judgment "as the good hand of my God was upon me" (Neh. 2:8),
"very clearly" (Deut. 27:8), in the city of Maaziah-Tiberias, "the
renowned city" (Ezek. 26:17), as it was understood by the congregation
of Prophets, the chosen of the Lord, the saints of our God, who
understand all hidden things and clarify the secret of wisdom, "the
oak-trees of righteousness" (Isa. 61:3), the men of the covenant, who
have concealed nothing of what was given to them nor added one word to
what was transmitted to them, who have made the Twenty-four Books of the
Scriptures powerful and mighty and they have established them in their
faith with accents of understanding, with specification of
pronunciation, with sweet palate, with beauty of speech...)

It is absolutely clear that the sentence upon which Graetz based
his argument contains not the slightest hint that its author was in any
way opposed to the Oral Law and merely means that the words of the
Prophets were not their own but by Divine Spirit, much as the sages of
the Midrash put it, "the Prophets received everything that they were to
prophesy in every generation from Mt. Sinai". (Exodus Rabbah 28:6; a
similar thought is expressed in a homily in T.B. Berakhot 5a). Even the
expression אילי הצדק is merely a biblical metaphor (Isaiah 61:3) and
contains no Karaite allusion. We have already seen other expressions
(מלמד, משכיל) which, although used by Karaites, were perfectly

acceptable to the Rabbanites as well, and this expression, too, was used by Rabbanites[135] and is indeed very apt in its context, i.e., describing the Prophets by a prophetic metaphor.[136] Generally it should be made clear that the fact that the Karaites adopted a biblical expression is not evidence that everybody who used it was a Karaite; particularly in the early generations.

It is therefore impossible to grasp at the Karaism of Moses Ben Asher in order to better establish that his son was also a Karaite.

1.3.2.   We will now examine the evidence that Graetz derived from the colophon of MSA. At first glance it would appear that Graetz was justified. The codex was handed over for safekeeping into Karaite hands (1.3.0.2.1); Israel of Baṣra was a Karaite (1.3.0.2.3); and the Rabbanite dedication is a later addition (1.3.0.2.4). However, once again Graetz ignored one "detail": all these facts are derived from a colophon that was written after Aaron Ben Asher's death and which in fact mentions him eulogistically. One cannot therefore attribute to Ben Asher the religious beliefs of the author of the colophon.

Above we suggested three possibilities to explain how a manuscript could come into Karaite hands even in the lifetime of its Rabbanite scribe. In the case of Aaron Ben Asher there is no need to even enter into such a discussion. Manuscripts of the Bible changed owners frequently - from Rabbanite into Karaite hands and vice versa.[137] Whether MSA passed into Karaite hands during his lifetime or after it, Ben Asher may not even have known of it.

I will not treat here the problem of whether the evidence of the colophon is true insofar as it relates to Ben Asher; suffice it to say that there are those who reject it.[138] For the purpose of this discussion I have assumed that the statements in the colophon are reliable; if they are not, and Aaron Ben Asher did not in fact point the

codex, Graetz's arguments are, of course, completely baseless. Today
it can be stated with a fair degree of certainty that MSA was not
pointed by the proper hand of Ben Asher[139] and that the evidence of the
colophon in this respect is, therefore, untrustworthy.

That the codex was first in Rabbanite hands is indicated by the
express condition laid down by the dedicator: "Should any Rabbanite Jew
(איש מכל זרע ישראל מבעלי הבינה מהרבנים) desire on any day of the year
to see in it (the codex) matters of *plene* or defective spelling ... or
any of the accentuation signs they should take it (the codex) out to
him to see, study and understand - but not to read or preach from - and
then they should return it to its place..."[140] This means that
although the codex was meant for public reading in the Karaite
synagogue on the three festivals only, as is previously specified in
the colophon, the owners were still obliged to show it to the
Rabbanites for the purpose of comparison on any day of the year. It
seems reasonable that this was not just a manifestation of good will on
the part of the Karaites but rather an explicit condition made by the
vender at the time of the sale. It is highly unlikely that such a
condition would have been made by anyone other than a Rabbanite.

The phrase "to see, study and understand but not to read or preach
from" reveals the function the codex performed amongst Rabbanites and
the purpose for which it was written. Collected books of the Bible,
vocalized and with accentuation signs (such as MSA and MSC) were used
by Rabbanites for study purposes only and not for public reading or
preaching. They were indeed written for the former purpose. The
condition that Rabbanites use it only for study and comparison is not a
limitation, as Graetz understood it (1.3.0.2.2),but rather an expression
of the main purpose for which it was written. Thus Graetz's argument[141]
that a Rabbanite would never have written the entire Bible in one volume

with vowels and accents for public synagogue reading is void.
Furthermore, no Rabbanite would copy the Bible in codex form (i.e., in
book form as opposed to scroll form) for public reading.[142] There was
only one use for pointed codices with Masora attached and that was for
comparison with other books and for study.

We have now finished the discussion of the main arguments put
forward to prove that Aaron Ben Asher was a Karaite.[143]

2.   THE PROOFS THAT BEN ASHER WAS A RABBANITE

2.1. The Attitude of the Rabbanites

The basic - and strongest - counter argument which was made
against the suggestion that Ben Asher was a Karaite was the fact that
Maimonides accepted Ben Asher's version of the Bible, from which it
follows that he also accepted Ben Asher himself. Maimonides writes
(*Yad ha-Ḥazaqa, Hilkhot Sefer Tora*, 8:4):

"The book (codex) upon which we have relied in all these
matters[144] is the famous book in Egypt, which includes the 24 books (of
the Bible), and which was in Jerusalem some years ago for the purpose
of correcting other books according to it; all relied on it because
Ben Asher corrected and worked on it (ודקדק בו) many years and examined
it many times according to the tradition. I relied on it for the Tora
scroll which I wrote according to the *halakha*."

Against this serious and basic contradiction to their views, which
many scholars raised,[145] those who supported the theory that Ben Asher
was a Karaite could make one of two answers: Either Maimonides was not
aware that Ben Asher was a Karaite and thus erred unknowingly, or
Maimonides did know that Ben Asher was a Karaite but was prepared to
rely on the version of a Karaite heretic.

Graetz half-heartedly hinted at the first possibility when he
wrote[146] that "something strange happened" (*etwas Wunderliches
passiert*) to Maimonides. It is, however, impossible that Maimonides
did not know such a fact. Books with Ben Asher's pointing were common
at that time and it seems that Ben Asher as a person was famous. Had
there been even the slightest doubt about his orthodoxy or the

slightest hint of any leaning towards Karaism Maimonides would not have relied on him.

Pineles, who accepted the second possibility, completely rejects the first. It is inconceivable, in his view, that all the Tora scrolls, from that time until today, are u n w i t t i n g l y based on the version of a heretic. However, although Pineles disagreed with Graetz's view at first and was the first to come out against some of his proofs,[147] he ultimately changed his mind.[148] He accepted Graetz's position and attempted to prove that Maimonides k n o w i n g l y relied on Ben Asher although he was a Karaite; because he did not see Ben Asher's Karaism as disqualification for writing a Tora scroll according to the *halakha*. To this end Pineles cited proofs from the *halakha*, in particular Simeon ben Gamliel's statement: "In those commandments which the *Kutim* (כותים: Samaritans) do observe they are more particular than Jews." (T.B. Gittin 10a). An anonymous author[149] demolished this argument with several apt points which seem to be perfectly reasonable, and demonstrated that it is impossible to draw Pineles' conclusion from the *halakha* and that Maimonides would certainly not have relied on Ben Asher had he known him to be a Karaite.[150]

Furthermore, Maimonides was known for his extremism in uprooting any vestige of Karaitic influence that might have infiltrated Rabbanite laws and customs in some communities in such matters as, e.g., the status of women after childbirth, menstruant women and immersion.[151] It is entirely inconceivable that he would have relied on a Karaite in a matter so important and principal as the true version of the Bible.

No acceptable answer has been put forward to explain this fact: all the arguments for Ben Asher's Karaism are mostly just that - arguments; whereas against them stands the undeniable, clear historic fact that Maimonides, who lived only about two hundred years after Ben Asher, relied on him and accepted his version. Maimonides himself had many opponents who disagreed with his methods and parts of his theology; none of them, however, ever attacked him for having relied on Ben Asher, which they certainly would have done if they had had the slightest suspicion of Ben Asher.

Furthermore, no Rabbanite has ever accused Ben Asher of Karaism or objected because of it, even in the slightest degree, to his authority in matters of pointing and Masora. Nor do any of the Rabbanites, both grammarians and others, who mention him refer to him as a Karaite. Many of the early sages mention Ben Asher, among them Hai Gaon,[152] Ibn Janāḥ,[153] and particularly David Qimḥi[154] - whether it was his known work, DQHT, or another work[155] - it is reasonable to assume that these and other scholars would not have made use of it - at least not without clearly stated reservations - had they suspected even a taint of Karaism.

It cannot be argued that the Rabbanites considered the Karaites to be authorities in Masora and grammar and that therefore they were prepared to rely on Ben Asher. The Karaites considered themselves such experts and were proud of it, but the Rabbanites never saw them as such at all. Thus, for example, the author of *Ancient Questions in the Bible* attacks the Karaites and mocks their devotion to technical details (he calls them "doters on accents" עוגבי הטעמים)[156] while they lack a real, deep understanding of the Bible. Saadia Gaon also denied their expertise in matters of Masora[157] and one Rabbanite provoked them with unanswerable grammatical questions: "... and if you do not have a solution to these two words how can you call yourselves 'Masters of the Scriptures and Teachers'? For you do not know the reasons of vocalization and accentuation or the variations of the Twenty-four Books."[158] In later generations this attitude developed and became an absolute denial of the Karaites' linguistic abilities. Thus, Abraham ibn Ezra, in the introduction to his commentary to the Pentateuch, writes: "Devious people have chosen the second way ... and this is the way of the heretics

(הצדוקים) such as Anan and Benjamin, and Ben[159] Mashiaḥ and Yeshuᶜa and
all heretics, who do not believe in the words of the sages(מעתיקי הדת).[160]
And each person interprets the verses according to his whim and tends
either right or left also in the matter of the commandments and laws.
They lack any knowledge of the Hebrew
language and therefore make mistakes
in grammar. How then can they rely on their own opinions in
matters of the commandments when they are continually changing from side
to side according to their state of mind..."[161]

It is therefore inconceivable that Rabbanites would accept the
system of a Karaite for the version of the Bible; not only out of
suspicion of heresy, but also because he would be, as far as they are
concerned, completely unreliable in matters of language and grammar.

2.2. The Attitude of the Karaites

The Karaites never - and this was particularly true in Saadia's
time - attempted to conceal their religious beliefs; to the contrary,
they publicly proclaimed them and boasted of them in their writings.
They also lost no opportunity of reviling the Rabbanites and attacking
them even in works that did not deal with questions of *halakha*. Even
David ben Abraham, who wrote mainly of linguistic matters, continually
dehigrates the Rabbanites[162] and announces his pride in his own faith.
Had Ben Asher been a Karaite, he would not have been afraid to announce
the fact or, at least, to leave a broad hint to the effect in his
writings.

There is also no evidence that any Karaite at any time, ever claimed
that Ben Asher was a fellow believer; he is not mentioned in the lists of
Karaite sages[163] or in the memorial prayer in the Karaite prayer-book.[164]
The Karaite tendency to "adopt" Rabbanite scholars is well known; they

even claimed that Judah ben Quraysh and others were Karaites. They never, however, attempted to "adopt" Ben Asher.

When the Karaite, Caleb Afendopolo, at the end of the 15th century, attempted to decide in the question of alternative readings between the two great authorities, he decided in favour of Ben Asher's readings not on religious-theological grounds, but purely because of the great authority that had become Ben Asher's in the course of the centuries. He wrote:[165] "The opinion of Ben Asher is more correct than that of Ben Naftali. Although we follow Ben Naftali in the reading of some words and in some cases of vocalization and accentuation, in the great majority we follow Ben Asher." He brings a homily to support him: "The word Asher is from מאשרי העם (Isaiah 9:15; "the honest leaders of the people"), meaning righteousness and truth, whereas Naftali is from עקש ופתלתול (Deuteronomy 32:5; "perverse and crooked"). At a later time another Karaite, Mordecai ben Nisan (end of the 17th century), decided in favor of Ben Naftali:[166] "We rely on the reading of Ben Naftali; that is the tradition of our teachers from generation to generation." This might have been because he already considered Ben Asher a Rabbanite authority. The Karaite scholar of the last century, Abraham Firkovitch, never considered Ben Asher to be a Karaite until Pinsker and Graetz suggested it, at which time he was delighted to agree with them and annex another important sage to his own sect.

However a section in *Ḥilluq ha-Qaraʾim we-ha-Rabbanim*, attributed to Elijah ben Abraham, a Karaite of the 12th century,[167] has been seen as evidence by some scholars that Ben Asher was a Rabbanite;[168] other scholars see in it the opposite.[169] To clarify the matter we hereby present the section in question:[170]

ועוד ראו[171] חלופי מערבאי ומדנחאי בתורה זה אומר בכה וזה אומר בכה, מה שילמוד זה חסר ילמוד זה מלא, ומה שילמוד זה מלא ילמוד זה חסר, מה שילמוד זה תיבה אחת ילמוד זה שתי תיבות, מה שילמוד זה במסורת[172] ילמד זה בטעם, וכן

מסורת הרבה אחד למערבאי ואחד למדנחאי, מענהו לבן אשר ולבן נפתלי, וראה

במלת יששכר כי בן אשר יקראו יִשָּׂשכָר, ובן נפתלי יִשָּׂשכָר, ומשה (.ms ובן משה)

בן מוחה יִשָּׂשכָר וכאלה רבים, וכמו כן נכתבים דביונים חריונים, עפולים

טחורים, וכאלה רבים, עתה אם בדברים הנכתבים ונמסרים מפי הנביאים נתחלפו,

א"כ שאר הדברים והתורות אשר לא נכתבו מפי נביאים וחוזים, ק"ו שלא יכתבו

וישתבשו כאלה וכאלה, אף מקובל לומר יש אם למקרא ויש אם למסורת, ופירשו לא

תענה על ריב, על רב, על פי, על פה, אותם אתם, לעולם לעלם, ציצת ציצית

וכאלה רבים, ויכשר לתמים דעים שיתן לנו תורה עומדת בשתי הסעפים ולשתי

דיעות, והאם למסורת תהדוף והמסורת לאם ...

The author is attempting to undermine the whole basis of Rabbanism with one principal argument: How is it possible for there to be a difference of opinion with regard to the text of the Bible and its interpretation?[173] Is it conceivable that God would have given an ambiguous Torah? The Rabbanites interpret the text in two ways: sometimes they follow the text as it is pronounced (יש אם למקרא) and sometimes as it is written (יש אם למסורת) for which the author cites examples. His conclusion is that the Bible as the Rabbanites have it has been corrupted and is therefore unreliable. He adds later: "And you do not believe us (ולנו לא תאמינו[174]; variant reading [175]תאמינו) because we are the descendants of the oppressed but we are earlier (i.e., more authentic) than your brothers (i.e., the Rabbanites)."

Thus regarding the interpretation of the text; the same is true for its version as well. The Karaites never accepted the view that there can be variant readings in the Bible; as far as they were concerned there can only be one correct version. Qirqisānī elaborated on this point and maintained that it is impossible that the two readings, the western and the eastern (מערבאי ומדנחאי), can both be correct but that only the western, that of Palestine, is correct; the Babylonian tradition is wrong.[176] Our author also mocks the Rabbanites about this matter - "one

says it this way and the other says it that way"[177] - and thus
demonstrates that the text of the Bible has been greatly corrupted
amongst the Rabbanites. He follows this with the further conclusion
that if this is the case with regard to the Bible ("matters which have
been committed to writing and handed down from the prophets") how much
more so must it be the case with regard to the Oral Law ("the other
matters and laws which were not committed to writing from the mouths of
the prophets").

Our author, however, was mistaken in one matter, a mistake in which
he is not unique: he identifies the variant readings of the Palestinian
and Babylonian traditions with those of Ben Asher and Ben Naftali. It
appears that he was not expert in grammar and Masora and when he wanted
to give examples of the variant readings of Palestine and Babylonia, as
he had done for the text as read and written, he described them as
מענהו (=.i.e) לבן אשר ולבן נפתלי and cited an example of   t h e i r
variant readings. The main point at issue between Ben Asher and Ben
Naftali is not in matters described by our author - *plene* and defective
spellings or whether a word is to be written in one word or two - but in
vocalization and accentuation, especially in *Ga'ya* notation. The actual
vocalization[178] of our author's examples[179] and the issue of *qere* and
ketiv that he discusses[180] (דביונים, חריונים etc.) raise serious doubts
about his knowledge of these subjects.

However, this mistake is of value to us for by it he reveals his
attitude to Ben Asher and Ben Naftali most clearly. He identifies their
versions with the Palestinian and Babylonian with the result that their
variant readings are, to him, a symbol for the corruption of the
Rabbanites. He certainly considered both Ben Asher and Ben Naftali
exemplary Rabbanites.

2.3. <u>Masoretic and Grammatical Methods</u>

2.3.0.   It is only fitting to compare the Karaite views of Masora and

grammar with those of the author of DQHT, even though it is now

clear that most of the sections of that work which are discussed here and

from which proofs are brought to prove Ben Asher's Rabbanism, do not

really belong to DQHT. It has been demonstrated in my edition of that

work (Dotan 1967) that paragraphs 4, 5, 9, 10, 16, 36 and 71, which are

discussed in the following pages, are not part of DQHT and cannot be

attributed to Ben Asher, and that no proof can be deduced from them for

either Ben Asher's Rabbanism or Karaism.

However, since the purpose of this study is also to reflect the

h i s t o r y of the controversy and since, in the previous chapter, we

did not rule out of the discussion the points put forward for Ben Asher's

Karaism on the basis of these and other paragraphs about which there can

be no doubt today that they are not Ben Asher's, we will also discuss here

the proofs for his Rabbanism based on them. Thus our opinion of the

original scope of DQHT does not have to be connected to the arguments put

forward here to prove that Ben Asher was a Rabbanite; the acceptance of

that latter conclusion is not conditioned by the acceptance of the former.

For the sake of convenience, we have not changed the old terminology

and will continue to refer to these paragraphs as DQHT, although it is

clear that they are not part of that work.

2.3.1.   The attitude of the Karaites to the vocalization and the

accentuation marks of the Bible is well known. As Judah Hadassi put it:[181]

"Tora scrolls should be marked with both the vocalization and

accentuation ... for God would not have given them (i.e., the scrolls)

without the vocalization and accentuation ... for the writing of God was

graven on the Tablets so they were complete in script with vocalization and accentuation ..."

If we compare the attitude reflected in DQHT we find a completely
different view both with regard to vocalization and with regard to
accentuation.

2.3.1.1. *Vocalization*. The author of DQHT on several occasions points
out that the 22 letters were divinely given through Moses   נתונות משמי
שפרה, מפי הגבורה, על יד עָנָו נקרא(§4);משמים אתוריות, על יד עָנָו קנויות (§5);
ממשה קנויות (*ibid*.), but does not include the vocalization or the
accentuation. To the contrary, when he discusses the peculiar attributes
of the guttural letters, אחה"ע (§5), which can take two vowel signs at
once (i.e., the *ḥaṭefs*) he particularly stresses that this attribute is
not intrinsic to the letters but is because of the additional
vocalization which was learned from the prophets and *soferim* (scribes):

כי כל אותיות, אשר ממשה קנויות, כל אות מלך אחד לבדו לו, משרתו בדרך אחד

שבילו, בנועם דבור מלולו, חוץ מן אחה"ע הידועים, אשר במקרא קבועים, כי

שני כתרים, נחלו בארבעה ועשרים ספרים, כלמוד נביאים וסופרים (§5)

namely, that each of the letters אחה"ע has two crowns - two vowel signs -
which is the teaching of the prophets and scribes. Also in his
introduction to the vowel inventory he points out that the seven vowels
"are from the Prophets" (מנביאי עתידות; §10).

It is difficult to establish precisely to whom he attributed the
origin of the vocalization signs - the Prophets or the *soferim* (and see
below) - but two basic lines of thought are clear which are in absolute
opposition to the Karaite view: that the letters and the vocalization
signs did not come from the same source, and that the vocalization did not
originate at Sinai.

Klar[182] found support for the view that Ben Asher believed that the
vocalization originated at Sinai in §9 of DQHT:

ידע הדורש בדעה גמורה ... כי כל המקרא שלם בלי חֲסֵרָה, כי נְקֻדָּה זְעֵירָה

תעמוד במקום האות כקורה, תועיל וּסֶבֶר תסבירה, וחסרון האות תגדורה

This means that the words which are defective(in spelling) are not really so because the vocalization comes instead of the missing *matres lectionis*, such as in עֶצֶר, חָצָה, נֹב, שָׁלֹה, etc. To the natural question "what reason can there be for vocalization of *plene* words in the same way as defective words" (מה טעם נקְדה על מלה יתרה כמו דרך מלה חסרה), namely, if the vocalization is intended to fill the deficiency of the *matres lectionis*, why is it that *plene* words were vocalized as well, the DQHT answers that "the vocalization is a lesson and a warning (למוד ואזהרה) for students of Scripture that they should not err in reading between נגרא and נורא (Daniel 3:6) or between שׂורה (Isaiah 28:25) and סגרה (Judges 4:18) or between צגר and צוֹר (the city) or between עגר (Daniel 2:35) and עוֹר (skin)." Klar concludes: "The answer is not really an answer because if we rely on the vocalization the whole Tora could have been written defective; but it is not relevant to our matter."

Klar was wrong. It *is* relevant to our matter, and the answer is an answer; only the conclusion is wrong because it was drawn on the assumption that the author believed that vocalization originated at Sinai. However, from the passage we see that this assumption is incorrect, for had the author so believed he could not have given that answer. The only purpose of the whole discussion is to clarify the term חסר ("deficient") which is frequently found in masoretic works and which is earlier mentioned (בה חֲסֵרָה ויתרה כאָמֶר זקני חבורה) and to rule out the literal translation which suggests that something is missing. The purpose of the vocalization is, on the one hand, to replace the *matres lectionis* which are not written and, on the other, to prevent mistakes in the reading of *plene* words ("A lesson and a warning for students of the Tora[183] that they should not err in reading between נורא and נגרא"). The vocalization is, thus, not equal in value to the consonantal text; it

only comes to complement it. This is what the DQHT was driving at and it
is a view completely contradictory to the Karaite. A Karaite does not
have to explain vocalization and justify its need; as far as he is
concerned, letters and vowels are one.

Klar[184] also attempted to derive that according to the author of
DQHT the Tora was given with both vocalization and accentuation from the
sentence (§9): "It (the Tora) was handed down with letters and words,
innumerable (vocalization) points, and well defined accents and grammar."
(‏באותיות ותיבות מסורה, ונקֻדות עד לאין ספירה, ובטעמים ובדקדוק גדורה‎).
However, his conclusion is not justified. This sentence does not relate
to the beginning of the chapter (§9) "At first God gave the Ten
Commandments ..." and does not mean that the letters and the vocalization
originate at Sinai; its author does not say that and never intended to.
He is discussing the text of the Bible in his role of masorete, i.e., the
Bible with its letters, vocalization and accentuation(‏בטעמים ובדקדוק‎[185]
‏גדורה ובשבעה מלכים אזורה‎) exactly as he does elsewhere (§3),[186] and it
is about this text that he says it was handed down, not from Sinai, but
"as the speech of the assembly elders and the statement of the Tora's
soferim" (§9; ‏כְּאֹמֶר זקני חבורה ומאמר סופרי תורה‎), i.e., by the masoretes.

2.3.1.2. *Accentuation.* The position of DQHT with regard to the
accents is clear; they were not given at Sinai but rather (§16) "out of
the mouth of the (understanding) teachers and the *soferim*" (‏מפי מבינים‎
‏וסופרים‎).This idea is repeated several times with open reference to the
rabbinic homily to Nehemiah 8:8: the words ‏וְשׂוֹם שֶׂכֶל‎ (giving sense)
allude to accents (T.J. Megilla 4:1 74d).In §4 our author states:

‏עוד שנים עשר טעמים, המשולים במי אגמים ... נגון נואמים, שיר מנעימים,‎
‏בשום שכל חתומים, מפי נבונים וחכמים ...‎

and in §17:

‏שער הטעמים שנים עשר רשומים ... בפי נבונים וחכמים, בשום שכל חתומים‎

In the colophon of MSC,[187] Moses Ben Asher calls the accents טעמי שכל,
an expression based on the aforementioned homily, and not only does he
allude to a rabbinic source in DQHT, but again hints that the accentuation
was handed down from "the mouth of the understanding and the wise" and not,
as the Karaites believed, to Moses at Sinai.

It appears that DQHT distinguishes between the tradition of
accentuation which is (§16) "tested, refined, out of the mouths of Prophets
and sages and the knowledgeable and the intelligent, sealed with the seal
of God's Prophets"[188]

(בחונים מזֻקָּקים, מפי נביאים וחכמים, ויודעים ומשכילים, חתומים בחותם נביאי אל)

and between the actual graphic accentuation marks which came from the
elders of the Sanhedrin (§16): "Eight are marked (bound, linked) above and
four (bow) below, they give reason and do not fear ... they are fixed by
the elders of the Circle, the princely prophets of the Exile."

(שמונה למעלה עקודים, וארבעה למטה קדים, נותנים טעם ולא פוחדים, ומגביהים

ורדים, מְתֻקָּנִים מזקני עגלה, נביאי שרי הגולה)

Of the 12 accentuation signs used in the 21 Prose Books of the Bible,
eight are marked above the word and four below and these, the graphic
symbols, were designed by "the elders of the circle".

The phrase "elders of the circle" is an allusion to the talmudic
statement that "the Sanhedrin was like a half a circular threshing floor"
(סנהדרין היתה כחצי גורן עגולה; Sanhedrin 4:3) to which should also be
compared "who, in a circle, raised teachers" (אשר בעגולה גידל דורשים;
Soferim 19:7). This phrase was also in use in the period under discussion.
Thus an anonymous Rabbanite describes the Sanhedrin as "The wise men of the
circular threshing floor ..."[189] (חכמי גורן עגולה, חבורת הצדק הקדושה,

שוקדים על דלתות תלמוד ומשנה) and an ancient lament on the destruction of
the Palestinian communities tells that "honor was exiled from Israel and
the elders of the circle ceased" (מישראל כבוד גלה ושבתו זקני עגולה[190]).

In DQHT (§16) the phrase is used as a name of honor for the members of
the Sanhedrin; a phrase which would have no place in the mouth of a
Karaite.

In the light of the above we can assume as well that the dual
attribution of the vocalization - to the Prophets and to the *soferim*[191] -
is also based on a differentiation between the traditional pronounciation
(or the tradition of vocalization) which presumably originated with the
Prophets and the graphic symbols of vocalization which came from the
soferim.

The view that the graphic symbols for the vocalization and
accentuation were given at Sinai is an essential one for the Karaites,
not only because of the sanctity and halakhic authority which they
attribute to the vocalization, which is as important as the consonantal
text, but also in order to maintain their historic claim that they split
off from the Rabbanites before the times of the Mishnah and the Talmud.
For if they were to agree that the vocalization and accentuation were
fixed in that period - as DQHT expressly states regarding the accents -
or after it, their claim for antiquity would be untenable[192] since their
vocalization and accentuation are not different from the Rabbanite.
DQHT's view in this is clear and must be Rabbanite.

2.3.2.   Another matter in which DQHT's view is different from the
              Karaite is the following: The early Karaite grammarians see
the imperative as the basic form of the verb. The reason for this is not
clear;[193] it is, however, not by chance, for it is a constant trait in
the works of Karaite grammarians and commentators. David ben Abraham,[194]
Japheth ben ʿAlī,[195] Abū Al-Faraj Hārūn[196] and ʿAlī ben Sulaymān[197] all
mention it, and Harkavy[198] has published a manuscript fragment with
examples of verbs in the imperative form and paradigms with the imperative
as the base.[199]

The view of DQHT (§36) is completely different; it says:

... או זמן יפול על השם וְיֵעָשֶׂה פּוֹעֵל, ויבדיל בו עבר מן הנצב[200] ומן
הֶעָתִיד, כי הזמן על שלשה דרכים, עבר ונצב ועתיד ... כן. תאמר בעבר
דְּבַּרְתִּי ... ותאמר על הזמן הנצב דֹּבֵר ... .ותאמר על הזמן העתיד...[201]
דַּבֵּר ... יְדַבֵּר ...

The imperative-future is the last in his list and thus constitutes a
fundamental digression from the Karaite view.

The conclusions which follow from the clarification of the Rabbanite
views reflected in DQHT show that its author was not a Karaite. If the
author of the relevant sections was Aaron Ben Asher[202] then it is clear
that Aaron Ben Asher was not a Karaite.

2.3.3. From the marginal notes in MSC of Moses Ben Asher it follows
that he too was not a Karaite. In this manuscript there
appears several times the note:[203] י"ח מלין (בקרי) תיקון סופרי וחכמ' (18
words (in the Bible) are corrections of the *soferim* and sages). The
source of this list of 18 words is in a rabbinic midrash[204] which the
Karaites do not accept. Graetz[205] argued that the 18 scribal corrections
are an ancient tradition which used to be copied on biblical manuscripts
before the start of Karaism; the Karaites did not change the custom and
continued to copy the corrections. This, however, is a weak answer, for
it is exceedingly strange that a scribe of Moses Ben Asher's standing
would copy in his Bible notes which he did not accept or believe,
something which one would expect from an ignoramus. Furthermore, since
when did the Karaites respect ancient traditions? Did they not reject
the Oral Law which is certainly as ancient as the scribal corrections?
There is also explicit evidence that the Karaites did not accept the
scribal corrections in Qirqisānī's book, which contains a whole chapter
to explain the untenability of the Rabbanite view[206] on this point. A

masoretic note which appears at the end of the list of the 18 corrections
states:

אלו י"ח דברים תקון סופרים ודקדוקיהן משובחים, ומארה תבא על כל מי
שעליהם שטנה כותבים[207]

(These are the 18 praiseworthy corrections of the scribes; may a curse
come on anybody who denigrates them). This note is undoubtedly aimed at
the Karaites and denigration such as that of Qirqisānī.

2.4. Terms and Expressions

Although great care is needed when taking parallel language usage
into consideration, it is impossible to ignore the wealth of rabbinic
expressions, metaphors and phrases which are to be found in DQHT. Scholars
have already pointed out many such parallels from which it is obvious to
what extent Ben Asher was saturated by rabbinic language. We present here
just a few of the tens of such examples.[208]

The most important is the metaphor (§71):
והבטוי כהררים תלוים בשערה כשלהבת קשורה בגחלת the beginning of which is
found in Tractate Ḥagiga (1:8) and the end in *Séfer Yeẓira* (1:7).[209] The
phrase (§9) ובמסורות אשר הם סיג לתורה is coined after R. ʿAqiva's
statement (Avot 3:13): [210] מסורת (נ"יא מסורות) סיג לתורה. The talmudic
expression (§16) זקני עגולה has been discussed above (2.3.1.2.). DQHT's
warning (§9): ומן הדרך הזאת לא יסורה, ועל דברי חכמים לא יעבורה, ומצה וריב
וכל העובר על דברי חכמים חייב מיתה is close to יסירה, כי זאת דרך ישרה ...
(T.B. Berakhot 4b) or כל העובר על דברי סופרים חייב מיתה (T.B. ʿEruvin
21b) both from the point of view of the language and the content. Each
Karaite could investigate the law himself and thus the idea that it is
forbidden "to transgress the words of the sages" is foreign to Karaism.
The words of the Karaite sages themselves were given to change frequently
with different applications of logic[211] and this increased controversy

among them.   Perhaps the phrase ומצה וריב יסירה in DQHT is an allusion to
this state of affairs; the author admonishing the reader to forsake such
ways and to travel the straight, paved road of acceptance of the sages.

A similar thought is expressed in Moses Ben Asher's handwriting in
MSC. After he lists the Prophets according to rabbinic tradition he
states:[212] "All the Prophets of Israel from Moses ... until Daniel and
Malachi are one hundred and seventeen. From there on prophecy and
prophet cease. From there on incline your ear and listen to the words of
the sages."[213] There can be no doubt that he too accepted the Oral Law.
In another colophon to MSC[214] he also uses the typical mishnaic
expression מצורע מוסגר   (Megilla 1:7).[215]

3. WHO WAS THE KARAITE BEN ASHER ?

3.0.   From the time the Ben Asher controversy subsided, at the end of
the last century, our knowledge of Karaite literature has greatly
increased. Many manuscripts of Karaite works - Bible commentary, law,
lexicons, grammatical fragments - which were buried in *genizas* and
libraries, have come to light and been published in critical editions.
Thus a wider and more embracing view of this literature has become
possible. Manuscripts of an anti-Karaite polemic nature have also been
discovered and these too have contributed to research into Karaism.
Amongst these latter, Saadia Gaon's *Essa Meshali* (אשא משלי) is
particularly well known. It is a polemic against the Karaites and
particularly relevant to the subject we are discussing.

As various fragments of this work were discovered and published,
there was found written at the beginning of one of the fragments, before
the name of the work, an inscription in Arabic characters which scholars
found difficult to read or interpret. In 1943 the late Benjamin Klar
succeeded in reading the Arabic inscription correctly: אלרד עלי בן אשאר
עבראני "The responsum on Ben Asher; Hebrew".[216] This means that *Essa
Meshali* is Saadia Gaon's responsum against Ben Asher. To this should be
added the testimony of Dunash[217] that "he (Saadia Gaon) responded to Ben
Asher" (שהשיב על בן אשר) and the conclusion is that *Essa Meshali* is that
responsum. And since this work is a major attack on the Karaites, this
constitutes a strong argument to the effect that Ben Asher, against whom
the responsum was written, was a Karaite - a conclusion which seems to be
completely opposite to that which we have reached in our above discussion.

3.1. *Essa Meshali*

However, if we examine this new evidence in the light of what we
know of Ben Asher we will find several perplexing questions.

3.1.1.   Even those who believe that Ben Asher was a Karaite agree that
his Karaism is only reflected in scattered hints in his short
work, DQHT,[218] and these hints certainly are not of a polemical character
and were not made in order to prove the correctness of the Karaites'
claims; the author is merely stating his view - ·Karaite it is claimed -
in various masoretic matters. Is it conceivable that Saadia Gaon would
have written such a major[219] and detailed[220] work in answer to these few
scattered hints? Ben Asher, even according to the view that he was a
Karaite, did not attack the Rabbanites;[221] why then should Saadia choose
him as his target, particularly since there was no lack of influential,
aggressive Karaites in that period?

Lewin[222] has already pointed out: "It is extremely difficult to
decide that all the hard words in *Essa Meshali* - and they are many and
diverse - were aimed at Ben Asher alone even though the latter did not
make use of rabbinic interpretations in his DQHT." Later Lewin rejects
the assumption that Ben Asher was a Karaite, because his tradition would
not have been accepted by the Rabbanites over Ben Naftali's if that were
so. However, since Lewin did accept his predecessor's assumption with
regard to the *Essa Meshali* superscription, he was forced into explaining
that at first Saadia did write the work against Ben Asher, the masorete -
and thus the superscription - but afterwards expanded the work against
the Karaites. It is amazing that Lewin paid no attention to the fact that
Essa Meshali is a composition written according to a rigid stylistic plan
which has a predetermined number of 572 stanzas in a complicated

alphabetic acrostic form.[223] How would it be possible to "expand" such a composition?

Furthermore, it has never been proven that the superscription derives from Saadia himself; however, Lewin is assuming not only that, but also that it really belongs to the original shorter version and that Saadia copied it onto the later "expanded" version although it was no longer relevant to the content. It is inconceivable to attribute such absurdity to Saadia Gaon!

3.1.2.   All Ben Asher's activity was in the field of Masora and grammar. Saadia, however, deals[224] with such matters only peripherally[225] and even then not in a detailed manner but only generally, attacking the Karaites' exaggerated formal devotion to the masoretic signs. Even this attack is not couched in clear terms and it is obvious from it that it is aimed not at a specific person but at the whole Karaite community. Saadia would have had a lot to say against Ben Asher if the latter believed - as it is claimed - that vocalization originated at Sinai.

3.1.3.   If he disagreed with Ben Asher in matters of Masora and grammar because the latter was a Karaite, why does Saadia not mention him, even by the slightest hint, in one of his own grammatical works?

3.1.4.   *Essa Meshali* was composed as an attack on a typical Karaite who was a fanatic for his faith and who was one of the chief spokesmen for Karaism against the Rabbanites denigrating the sages of the Talmud; a Karaite who in Saadia's words "w r o t e that they (the Rabbanites) misled the Jews, deceitfully acquiring financial gain"[226] (כתב כי התעו איומה למען בצוע בצע בתרמה). Against such a Karaite there was a need to reply in order to demonstrate the foolishness of his - and his fellow Karaites' - claims. Saadia did not accuse them of an interest in

Masora and grammar - Saadia himself did a great deal in those fields - but
rather of their lack of understanding in these matters, and of the
absurdity of their interest seeing they do not accept rabbinic interpretation which is based on the peculiarities of the Masora and which
explains them.[227]

3.2.   The Superscription

However, I believe that Klar's reading of the superscription is
undoubtedly correct, as is Dunash's testimony, and that *Essa Meshali* was
written as a reply against Ben Asher. We are thus forced to say that
the composition was not addressed
against Aaron Ben Asher or his father,
Moses, the two great masters, but
against another Ben Asher, a Karaite
Ben Asher, who was, so to speak, a
"professional" Karaite, a belligerent
Karaite.   It must be borne in mind that neither Dunash nor the
Essa Meshali superscription mentions a personal name for Ben Asher, and
that it was only an assumption that the reference is to Aaron Ben
Asher the famous masorete, an assumption that was never questioned but
also never proved. It is in fact a baseless assumption[228] which was
accepted out of a mistaken preconception that in Saadia's generation the
unspecified name "Ben Asher" must refer to the famous masorete Ben
Asher;[229] Aaron Ben Asher, however, became famous in later generations
while in contemporary writings he is not so widely known.[230]
Who then is the Karaite Ben Asher whom Saadia Gaon was attacking?

3.2.1.   The obvious place to look is amongst the Karaite contemporaries
           of Saadia Gaon who attacked him. The Karaite sage, Sahl ben

Mazliaḥ, in one of his letters of reproach to Jacob ben Samuel, lists
Saadia's Karaite antagonists:[231]

ואתה עתה הטוב טוב אתה[232] מן סעדיה הפיתומי[233] ראש הישיבה הרוב
רב עם בני[234] מקרא יצ"ו[233] אם נלחום נלחם עמהם והלא חכמיהם ותלמידיהם
היו תובעים[235] ממנו לצאת אליהם ולשבת עמם[236] במלחמת[237] ה' ולערוך עמם
משפטיהם לדעת אי זה דרך הטוב מדרכיהם ואומרים משפט נבחרה לנו נדעה[238]
מה טוב בדבריהם, ולא רצה ומנע[239] נפשו לצאת[240] אליהם ובא חדר בחדר
להחבא, וגם לא היה מביא אליו כי אם את[233] אשר הוא חפץ, וגם[233] לא[241]
יכלו בני מקרא להקבץ עמו בשבת מפני הנר, ובן משיח הקציר נפשו מביניהם
והביא אותו חדר בחדר עד שצעק ואמר מה לי ולך לך מעלי, והספרים אשר כתב
לא הוציאם בחייו מתחת ידו על בני מקרא ואחד מהם נפל ביד בן משיח והשיב
עליו בחייו, וכן שלמון בן ירוחים[242] ע"ה[233] השיב עליו בלשון הקדש על אשר
כתב עליו[243], נשא[244] משלו[245] ואמר[246], ואחרי מותו כמות[233] נבל[233] נפלו
ספריו ביד בני מקרא[247] בכל מקום ומקום וישיבו עליו[248] תשובות בדברים
נכוחים כמסמרות[249] נטועים בספרים הרבה, כמו שעשה א ב ו א ל ט י י ב
ה נ ו ד ע א ל ג ב ל י[250], ו כ ן[251] ע ל י ב ן ח ס ו ן[252]
ו כ ן ב ן מ ש י ח ו ב ן י ר ו ח ם ה נ ו ד ע ב ן ר ו ח י ם,
ו א ב ו ע ל י ח ס ן[253] א ל ב צ ר י ו ז ו ל ת ם, ו ג ם
א נ י כ ת ב ת י ת ש ו ב ה ל ד ב ר י ו כ א ח ד מ ה ם, ו א ם
תבקש להתבונן היטב בספריהם עד אשר תמצא אמונת[254] הדבר ותדע כי האמת אתם.

"And now, are you better than Saadia, the Fayumite, the head of the
academy? Did he quarrel with, may God keep them, the Karaites? Did he
fight them? Their (i.e. the Karaite) scholars and students demanded that
he meet them and sit and discuss Godly matters with them to decide which
of their ways is the better ... and he (i.e., Saadia) refused and withheld
himself from going out to them and hid himself in the innermost room and
only permitted those whom he wanted to enter. The Karaites also could not
meet him on the Sabbath because of the (kindled) light. Ben Mashiaḥ,
however, separated himself from them and got in to him until he (Saadia)

cried, "What do you have to do with me? Leave me!" He did not publish[255]
in his lifetime the books that he wrote against the Karaites, but one fell
into the hands of Ben Mashiaḥ and he rebutted it in his (Saadia's)
lifetime. Also Salmon ben Yeruḥim, peace be on him, wrote a rebuttal in
Hebrew because he (Saadia) wrote *Essa Meshali*.[256] After his death, the
death of a villain, his books came into Karaite hands in all places and
they replied with correct, pointed statements in many books; as did Abū
al-Ṭayyib who is known as Al-Jabalī, as well as ʿAlī ben Ḥason, as well
as Ben Mashiaḥ, and Ben Yeruḥam who is known as Ben Ruḥim, and Abū ʿAlī
Ḥasan al-Baṣrī and others. I too, as one of them, also wrote a rebuttal
to his (Saadia's) words. Consider well their books until you find the
faith and you will realize that the truth is with them."

Of the five scholars mentioned in addition to Sahl himself, we have
more or less clear information about three; with regard to the other two,
Abū al-Ṭayyib al-Jabalī and ʿAlī ben Ḥason, our knowledge is very limited.

ʿAlī ben Ḥason, or Ben al-Ḥasan, was apparently the father of the
famous Japheth ben ʿAlī and he is mentioned by his grandson, Levi ha-Levi
ben Japheth, in the latter's introduction (מקדמא) to the weekly scriptural
reading, Devarim.[257]

Abū al-Ṭayyib al-Jabalī was not known of at all until George
Margoliouth[258] published the list of Karaite scholars of Ibn al-Hītī. In
that list Abū al-Ṭayyib al-Jabalī is mentioned by his Hebrew name,
S a m u e l   b e n   A s h e r   b e n   M a n ṣ ū r.

This is the relevant section:[259]

ואלשיך שמואל בן אשר בן מנצור אלמערוף באבו אלטייב אלג׳בלי כאן פי זמאן
אלשיך אבו[260] אלפרג׳ הארון ותנאטי׳רא[261] פי אלאביב ואלסנה אלשרעיה וכאן
עלי ראי אלמולי אבו עלי רח אֹת ולהו מקאלה פי אפסאד אלמחזור וחסאב אלמולד
ורד[262] עלי מנחם ראש מתיבא ענד וקופה עלי רקעה בן מנחם אלי אביתאבת איידה אֹת

"The sage, Samuel ben Asher ben Manṣūr, who is known as Abū al-Ṭayyib al-Jabalī, was in the time of the sage Abū al-Faraj Hārūn, and they argued about the spring and the year (as it is fixed) in *halakha*. And he was of the same opinion as the master, Abū ʿAlī, may God have mercy on his soul. And he has a treatise on the corruption of the calendric cycle and the reckoning of the *molad* (the conjunction of the moon with the sun). And he responded to Menahem, the head of the academy, when he found out about Ben Menahem's letter to Abū Tābit, may God help him."

Ibn al-Hītī's chronology is unreliable since, as stated above, Al-Jabalī is already mentioned in Sahl ben Maẕliaḥ's letter; if al-Jabalī was a contemporary of Abū al-Faraj Hārūn (who finished his *Kitāb al-Mushtamil* in 1026[263]) it is highly unlikely that Sahl would have known of him at all. We must therefore accept the testimony of Sahl, who was closer in time to Al-Jabalī, over that of Ibn al-Hītī, who lived in the 15th century. It can be estimated that Ibn al-Hītī discovered a work of Abū al-Faraj in which he argues with Al-Jabalī's   v i e w s   and assumed that they were contemporaries.

3.2.2.   Attention should also be paid to a difficulty in Sahl ben Maẕliaḥ in the above quoted passage. Abū al-Ṭayyib al-Jabalī is listed together with Karaites who responded to Saadia   a f t e r   his death. It is therefore impossible that he started the controversy with Saadia and that Saadia, according to the superscription, responded to him.[264]

However, if we take two points into consideration, we shall see that there is no contradiction and that the facts fit nicely.

3.2.2.1.   The Arabic word רד (and its Hebrew translation תשובה; responsum or answer) does not only mean a response to an attack that has been made or a question that has been asked; it can also mean a "reaction"

"denial" or "contradiction" to something that had not been either asked
as a question or posed as an attack or an opening of a debate. Thus, for
instance, Dunash wrote a book of תשובות against Saadia, who certainly had
not started a controversy with Dunash. What better example of this can
there be than Saadia's own composition, *Kitāb al-Radd ʿala ʿAnan* (The
Responsum against Anan); Anan lived more than 150 years before Saadia and
neither could have started a controversy with him or addressed a question
to him. Saadia could, thus, have written a reaction to Al-Jabalī; either
to one of the latter's works or to his Karaite preaching. Al-Jabalī,
according to Sahl, replied to this only after Saadia's death.

3.2.2.2. There is also another possibility. Al-Jabalī might have
actually started a controversy with Saadia and the רד of Saadia is an
actual response to it. In order to establish this possibility we will
have to examine some of the details in the passage from Sahl. There can
be no doubt that Sahl's testimony, insofar as the actual facts are
concerned, is truthful; i.e., that the scholars whom he lists did respond
to Saadia. However, his attempt to explain these facts by saying that
Saadia "hid himself in the innermost room" out of fear of his Karaite
opponents' sharpness is an attempt to cloak in a mantle of falshood the
grain of historic truth. A truth as bitter as gall to the Karaites'
pride, i.e., that, with the exception of the two most audacious, they did
not respond to Saadia during his lifetime. Sahl is not free of the
typical Karaite exageration and bombast which are clearly seen in his
letter. The exactness of his testimony is thus open to suspicion,
particularly the distinction he makes between those who answered Saadia
during his lifetime and those who did so after his death.

It appears that Sahl lists the scholars chronologically. Abū ʿAlī
Ḥasan al-Baṣrī - he is the famous Japheth ben ʿAlī - and Sahl ben Mazliah
himself are the youngest of the group and are thus mentioned at the end.

Ḥasan (or Ḥason)ben Mashiaḥ and Salmon ben Yeruḥim, who were contemporaries of Saadia, who disputed with him in his lifetime[265] (even according
to Sahl[266]) and of whom one actually faced Saadia, are listed before Abū
ʿAlī and Sahl. Of the first pair in the list, one is ʿAlī ben Ḥason,
the father of Japheth ben ʿAlī,[267] who was certainly older than the
others listed after him, and the other is Abū al-Ṭayyib al-Jabalī who is
at the head of the list. If the order is really chronological, as we
have tried to show, it is almost certain that the latter was the oldest
of them all.

Sahl's distinction between Saadia's contemporary and posthumous
responders is, therefore, strange and can only be accepted with
reservations. For if Ben Mashiaḥ and Salmon, who were younger than
Al-Jabalī, attacked Saadia during his lifetime, it is reasonable to
assume that Al-Jabalī also did so and that *Essa Meshali* was Saadia's
response to him. Such an inaccuracy in Sahl's letter may not have been
deliberate since the scholars listed lived in Babylonia,[268] Syria[269] and
Persia[270] - all far from Jerusalem, Sahl's domicile.[271] It is not
impossible that he erred in dating some of their compositions.

Al-Jabalī's dates need further investigation. Poznanski fixed him
at about the middle of the 10th century.[272] This date, however, is based
on identifying the Menahem, head of the academy, mentioned by Ibn al-Hītī,
with an otherwise unknown Menahem who posed questions to Saadia when the
latter was serving as Gaon,[273] as well as on Sahl's chronology the
relevant detail of which we have shown to be unreliable. The identification of Menahem, the head of the academy, is also very doubtful,[274] for
there was no head of an academy of that name in Saadia's time or after in
either Sura or Pumbedita. Therefore, Margoliouth's assumption[275] that
Menahem, the head of the academy, was the Gaon of Pumbedita in the second
half of the 9th century is very acceptable. If this is correct all the

details fit. Al-Jabalī lived in the time of this Menahem's son, i.e., at the end of the 9th century or the beginning of the 10th. He wrote a responsum against Menaḥem[276] and also other works in Karaite *halakha*, such as those Ibn al-Hītī mentions, and perhaps even polemical works. This literary activity for Karaism called for a response from the Rabbanites which was made by Saadia in *Essa Meshali*.[277]

Our suggestion above[278] with regard to the connection between Al-Jabalī and Abū al-Faraj Hārūn in Ibn al-Hītī's view can also be made with regard to his connection with Japheth ben ʿAlī who is mentioned by Ibn al-Hītī as "the master Abū ʿAlī". It is not necessary to assume from the passage that they were contemporaries - it is entirely possible that what Ibn al-Hītī saw of Al-Jabalī's work matched Japheth ben ʿAlī's views. Ibn al-Hītī did not know a great deal about Al-Jabalī and described his views by the simplest available method, i.e., he described the unknown person (Al-Jabalī) by the two known (Abū al-Faraj and Japheth); Al-Jabalī disagreed with Abū al-Faraj Hārūn and agreed with Japheth ben ʿAlī, although it is highly unlikely that any of the three ever saw either of the others.

3.2.3.   At any rate we have clearly demonstrated that Samuel ben Asher, who was known as Abū al-Ṭayyib al-Jabalī, was an active Karaite polemicist contemporaneous with (and perhaps older than) Saadia Gaon. From everything we know there is no reason why we should not assume that he was the Ben Asher against whom Saadia Gaon composed *Essa Meshali*. There can be no doubt that Al-Jabalī was an important Karaite in his time and one who "merited" such a response.[279]

4. THE VINE POEM

4.0. Hebrew Text and Translation

This study would not be complete if we did not discuss one more
piece of evidence that has been brought to prove that Moses Ben Asher was
a Karaite. At the end of MSL there is copied a poem about "Israel who is
compared to the vine". The poem consists of 23 lines of which the first
22 are an alphabetic acrostic and the last begins with the letter *kof*
which was apparently the last line of an acrostic spelling חזק. Zulay
discovered two other manuscripts of this poem: one comprised the first
eleven lines of the poem and the other comprised the continuation from
line 12 till line 22 and a further seven new lines which do not appear in
MSL, the last line of MSL being missing in this manuscript. The acrostic
of these seven new lines reads: משה בן אש (Moses Ben Ash). Klar
published the poem[280] according to these three manuscripts[281] and we
present here his text and vocalization.

זה הוא תפארת ישראל ותולדות הנביאים שישראל נמשלו בגפן ודליותיה

הם הנביאים ושרשיה הם האבות ויונקותיה הם החכמים מצדיקי הרבים

אַתָּה נְטַעְתָּה[282] גֶּפֶן שֹׂרֵקָה

מִשְׁפָּחָה הָיְתָה מִכָּל־גְּפָנִים[283]

בְּמִגְדַּל דָּוִיד הָיְתָה נְטוּעָה

וְאֶרֶז[284] מִלְּבָנוֹן הָיָה[285] בְּתוֹכָהּ

גֶּפֶן יְיָ שִׁבְטֵי יַעֲקֹב

וְאִישׁ יְהוּדָה נֶטַע שַׁעֲשׁוּעָיו

דָּלִיּוֹת הַגֶּפֶן הֵם הַנְּבִיאִים

וּמִגְדַּל דָּוִיד הוּא הַר צִיּוֹן

5 הָיְתָה שְׁתוּלָה עַל מַיִם רַבִּים

וַתִּגְבַּהּ מְאֹד בֵּין הָעֲבֹתִים

וְהַגֶּפֶן הַהִיא כְּפֹנָה שָׁרָשֶׁיהָ

וְעַל־מַיִם רַבִּים שִׁלְּחָה קְצִירֶיהָ

זְמֹרוֹת[286] הַגֶּפֶן חֲסִידֵי עוֹלָם

הֵם אַבְרָהָם יִצְחָק וְיַעֲקֹב

חַכְמֵי הַגֶּפֶן נְבִיאֵי עוֹלָם

מֹשֶׁה וְאַהֲרֹן וּמִרְיָם אֲחוֹתָם

טַרְפֵי הַגֶּפֶן יְהוֹשֻׁעַ וְכָלֵב

וְשִׁבְעִים זְקֵנִים וְאֶלְדָּד וּמֵידָד

10 יִקְּבֵי הַגֶּפֶן הֵם שְׁנֵי מִזְבְּחוֹת

וְהַהֵיכָל וּדְבִיר לִפְנִים לִפְנַי

כְּמַרְאֵה חָתָן וְכִדְמוּת כַּלָּה

כֵּן עֲדַת יְשֻׁרוּן נִגְּשָׁה לַחוֹרֵב

This is the adornment of Israel and the genealogy of the prophets
    for Israel is compared with a vine and its branches
are the prophets,and its roots are the Patriarchs and its young twigs
    are the sages who made the many righteous.

Thou hast planted a choice stock of vine
    praised more than all vines.

In the tower of David it was planted
    and a cedar of Lebanon was in its midst.

The vine of God are the tribes of Jacob,
    and the man of Judah is his beloved plantation.

The branches of the vine are the Prophets,
    and the tower of David is the mountain of Zion.

5 It was planted over great waters
    and was very lofty among the bushy trees.

And that vine bent its roots
    and sent out its sprays over great waters.

The branches of the vine are the pious of the world,
    they are Abraham, Isaac and Jacob.

The Sages of the vine are the Prophets of the world
    Moses and Aaron and Miriam, their sister.

The leaves of the vine are Joshua and Caleb
    and the Seventy Elders and Eldad and Medad.

10 The vine presses are two altars
    and the Temple and the Holy of Holies innermost.

Like the appearance of a bridegroom and the image of a bride,
    so did the community of Jeshurun draw near to Horeb.

לְלֻבֵּי [287] הַגֶּפֶן הָיָה שְׁמוּאֵל

אֵלִיָּהוּ וֶאֱלִישָׁע יְשַׁעְיָה וְיִרְמִיָה

מַבּוּעֵי הַגֶּפֶן הָיָה יְחֶזְקֵאל

וְהוֹשֵׁעַ וְיוֹאֵל עָמוֹס וְגַם-עֹבַדְיָה

נְבִיאֵי חָזוֹן יוֹנָה וּמִיכָה

נַחוּם חֲבַקּוּק וְגַם-צְפַנְיָה

15 סְמַדְרֵי [288] הַגֶּפֶן חַגַּי וּזְכַרְיָה

וּמַלְאָכִי וְגַם-אִישׁ חֲמֻדוֹת

עִנְּבֵי [289] הַגֶּפֶן הֵם בְּנֵי אַהֲרֹן

קְדוֹשֵׁי יְיָ מְשָׁרְתֵי אֱלֹהֵינוּ

פִּרְחֵי הַגֶּפֶן הֵם בְּנֵי לֵוִי

מְשׁוֹרְרִים כֻּלָּם בְּנֹעַם כִּגְזֹרוֹתֵיהֶם [290]

צִמְחֵי הַגֶּפֶן הֵם עוֹלָלִים

יוֹנְקֵי שָׁדַיִם אֲשֶׁר לֹא טָעֲמוּ חֵטְא

קָנֶה הָיָה סָמוּךְ [291] לַגֶּפֶן

הוּא דָוִד מֶלֶךְ יִשְׂרָאֵל

20 רַבִּים רְשָׁעִים הִכָּה דָוִד

בֶּאֱדוֹם וּמוֹאָב בְּעַמּוֹן וּפְלִשְׁתִּים

שָׁרְשֵׁי הַגֶּפֶן יוֹאָב וַאֲבִישַׁי

וַעֲשָׂהאֵל, וְעָשׂוּ כֻּלָּם כִּגְבוּרָתָם

תְּמִימֵי הַגֶּפֶן הֵם זִקְנֵי בְתֵירָה [292]

יוֹרְשֵׁי הַנְּבִיאִים יוֹדְעֵי בִינָה

The sprouts of the vine were Samuel,

    Elijah and Elisha, Isaiah and Jeremiah.

The sources of the vine were Ezekiel,

    Hosea and Joel, Amos and also Obadiah.

The Prophets of vision, Jonah and Micah,

    Nahum and Habakkuk and also Zephaniah.

15 The buds of the vine, Haggai and Zechariah

    and Malachi and also the man greatly beloved (Daniel).

The grapes of the vine are the sons of Aaron,

    the holy men of the Lord, the servants of our God.

The blossoms of the vine are the sons of Levi,

    all singers, with the sweetness of their harps.

The shoots of the vine are the children,

    those sucking the breasts, not having tasted sin.

A cane served as support of the vine

    that is David, the King of Israel.

20 Many evildoers has David smitten

    in Edom and Moab, in Ammon and the Philistines.

The roots of the vine are Joab and Abishai

    and Asahel who all acted in accordance with their might.

The perfect ones of the vine are the Elders of Bathyra,

    the heirs of the prophets, who are endued with understanding.

מַיִם עֲמֻקִּים מַבִּיעֵי חִיד[וֹ]ת

לְבָם מַשְׂכִּיל חָכְמָה כְּנַחַל נ[וֹבֵעַ]

שֶׁעַשׁוּעִים הִתְקִינוּ טַעֲמֵי מִקְרָא

בְּשׁוֹם שֵׂכֶל וְנִיב מְפֹרָשׁ

25   הִקִּיפוּ גָדֵר לְתוֹרַת אֱלֹהֵינוּ

מָסֹרוֹת סְדוּרוֹת לְ[הַחְפִּי]ם פֶּתִי

בֶּאֱמוּנָתָם יָסְדוּ פֵּרוּשׁ מִקְרָא

כְּלוּלִים בְּמִצְוֹת בְּלִי לָסוּר מִדֶּרֶךְ

נֶפֶשׁ נָתְנוּ עַל-תּוֹרַת אֱלֹהֵינוּ

לְהַצְדִּיק [רַ]בִּים לְהַגְדִּיל[293]   תּוֹרָה

אֵפְפוּם צָרוֹת מִמַּלְכֵי יְוָנִים

וְהִגְלוּ[ם] וְנִפְּצוּם [לְנ]א וּבְנוֹתֶיהָ

שִׁבְטֵי קְדוֹשִׁים נִתְעוֹרְרוּ[294]   עֲלֵיהֶם

וְחִנְּכוּ נֵרוֹת עַל-נְפִילָתָם

. . . .

. . . .

30   קָרֵב יְשׁוּעָה וְתַמְלִיךְ[295] הַגֶּפֶן

וְתַעֲקֹר שֹׁרֶשׁ כָּל-הַמַּמְלָכוֹת.

Deep waters that utter mysteries;

    their heart brings forth wisdom like a flowing brook.

As delights they have established the accents of Scripture,

    giving sense and distinct utterance.

25 They have erected as a fence round the Tora of our God

    well-arranged *Masoras* to instruct the ignorant.

In their faith they have established the interpretation of Scripture,

    surrounded by commandments without deviating from the path.

Their souls they have given for the Tora of our God

    to make the many righteous, to extend the Tora.

Afflictions surrounded them from the kings of the Greeks

    and they exiled them and dispersed them to No (Egypt) and its

    provinces.

The holy tribes rose up against them

    and dedicated lights (candles) on their fall.

    ....

      ....

30 Bring nearer   salvation, let the vine reign,

    pluck out the roots of all kingdoms.

4.1. Proofs that the Author was a Karaite

4.1.0.   From the fact that the poem discusses, *inter alia*, matters of
accentuation and *Masora*, Klar concluded that the final acrostic
is the name of Aaron Ben Asher's father, Moses. From the content of the
poem he concluded that it's author was a Karaite. The following are the
points upon which Klar based his conclusion that the poem was written by
a Karaite:[296]

4.1.0.1.   Although the poem reviews all the great figures of Jewish
history, it does not mention the Men of the Great Assembly (אנשי כנסת
הגדולה), neither Simeon the Pious nor the Pairs.

4.1.0.2.   The poem "exalts the Elders of (*Bene*) Bathyra, who did not
serve Shemaiah and Avtalyon and who disagreed with Hillel the Elder, the
most hated of the Rabbanites, to the level of heirs of the Prophets, and
attributes to them the institution of the biblical accents and Masora, as
opposed to the rabbinic sages who attribute accentual division and Masora
to Ezra and his associates (T.B. Nedarim 37b)". In this Klar sees "the
theory that the Karaites always maintained, i.e., the choosing of minority
opinions in the Talmud according to whom the *halakha* was not decided, in
order to attach themselves to early sages."

4.1.0.3.   In MSL the poem is preceeded by a prose superscription which
ends "its (the vine's) young twigs are the sages who made the many
righteous" (מצדיקי הרבים), a phrase which is repeated in the body of the
poem (line 27): "...to make the many righteous (להצדיק [ר]בים), to extend
the Tora". This phrase is used by Karaites, such as Japheth ben ʿAlī, to
describe their sages.

4.2. Refutation

However, none of these arguments can prove that the author was a Karaite.

4.2.1.   It seems that the chronological survey was not intended to exhaust either the Prophets and sages of Israel - Ezra and many of the prophets whom Moses Ben Asher himself lists at the end of MSC[297] are missing - or the great historical figures - Saul, Solomon and the Kings of Israel are missing as are other scriptural figures such as Nehemiah and Mordecai. Even if the author was a Karaite he should have listed the chain of tradition of the Karaites. The lack of continuity is as difficult to understand from the pen of a Karaite as much as it is from the pen of a Rabbanite, and the only conclusion to be drawn is that the author, Karaite or Rabbanite, did not intend to present a comprehensive historical survey.

The intention of the poet was to compare the People of Israel to the vine in the form of a homily[298] the source and basis for which we do not know. As long as this basis and its source remain unknown it cannot be claimed that the author deliberately ignored specific personages; nothing can be deduced from names which appear to us to be missing (they might even have appeared in the poem's continuation which is not extant) or from seemingly superfluous names, such as Joab and his two brothers, who are, from the point of view of the Jewish religion, not very important, or from the sons of Bathyra (see below).

4.2.2.   The Karaites believe that the vocalization and accentuation were handed to Moses at Sinai, and at any rate their religious principles could certainly not allow them to attribute the origin of vocalization and accentuation to the last generation of Pairs (זוגות).[299]

The fact that the poet does attribute them to the Elders of Bathyra[300]
(contemporaries of Hillel) is, therefore, a proof to the contrary. A
Karaite could never have written that.

While it is true that the Karaites tend to "adopt" sages according to
whose view, in the Talmud, the law is *not* decided, the Sons of Bathyra are
not a good example. They did not disagree with Hillel but rather asked
him a matter of law that they did not know. When Hillel enlightened them
they accepted and "they immediately set him at the head and made him their
נשיא (president)" - thus the Babylonian Talmud (Pesaḥim 66a); according to
the Jerusalem Talmud (Pesaḥim 6:1; 33a) they argued with him and "did not
accept his view until he said 'may it (i.e., a curse) come on me if I did
not hear the law from Shemaiah and Avtalyon.'" The sons of Bathyra did
not, it is true, serve (their apprenticeship with) Shemaiah and Avtalyon;
but they did respect their opinion and did not argue with them, for the
story in the Jerusalem Talmud continues "As soon as they heard that (i.e.,
that Hillel had heard the law from Shemaiah and Avtalyon) they immediately
appointed him their president". Furthermore, Rabbi Judah Ha-Nasi is
reported as saying, "I will do whatever anybody tells me except if it is
what the Elders of Bathyra did to my ancestor (Hillel), that they abdicated
and appointed him." (T.J. Ketubbot 12:3, 35a; Kilaim 9:4, 32b). Elsewhere
it is recorded: "There were three who relinquished their crowns in this
world and (thus) inherited the world to come: Jonathan, the son of Saul;
Elazar ben Azariah; and the Elders of Bathyra. With regard to Jonathan,
Rabbi (i.e., Judah Ha-Nasi) said, did not even the women behind the curtain
(i.e., in the harem) know that David was going to rule (i.e., Jonathan's
sacrifice was not so amazing), and in the case of Elazar ben Azariah (when
he was appointed to the presidency of the court in place of Simeon ben
Gamliel) a condition was made (that he later relinquish the presidency);
neither of these cases can be compared to that of the Elders of Bathyra

who relinquished the presidency and appointed him (i.e., Hillel)."
(T.J. Pesaḥim *Ibid.*; cf. T.B. Baḇa Meẓīa 85a).

The record in the Jerusalem Talmud must be understood properly.
There was no disagreement with Hillel; the Elders of Bathyra did not know
the law in question at all and hesitated to accept it on the basis of
Hillel's proofs alone. They cannot thus be considered a minority opinion
according to whom the law is not decided, particularly since Hillel was at
that time just "another Babylonian" and not president of the court whose
decision must be accepted. They themselves were in the latter position.
Furthermore, although they were in the majority (two to one) they did
ultimately accept his view.[301]

To this must be added the fact that although there are several
different Karaite theories of their chain of tradition - some start at
Rehoboam, the son of Solomon,[302] others at the Pairs,[303] Judah ben Tabbai,
Shemaiah, Shammai, and after them R. Johanan ben Zakkai, R. Eliezer ben
Hyrcanus and others - no Karaite attributes any importance to the Sons of
Bathyra or "adopts" them for any purpose whatsoever.[304]

4.2.3. All that was said above with regard to the terms מלמד[305]
משכיל[306] אילי הצדק[307] and applies to the term מצדיקי הרבים.
This biblical expression is no Karaite monopoly even if Japheth ben ʿAlī
did use it a few times. The term מצדיקי, close to that under discussion,
was used by Saadia in *Essa Meshali*,[308] and both are based on Daniel 12:3:
"And they that be wise (והמשׂכלים) shall shine as the brightness of the
firmament; and they that turn many to righteousness (ומצדיקי הרבים) as the
stars for ever and ever." The people of Fostat actually so described
Sherira Gaon in their letter to his son, Hai Gaon:[309]

פאר הישיבה שלגולה העתיק במחצות מצדיקי הרבים

It must be pointed out that, in principle, one cannot rely on

individual words, which appear to be Karaite terms, in order to establish
that the user was a Karaite. Only an investigation of the poem's content
can serve as a basis for any such assumption. What does such an
investigation reveal?

4.3. An Analysis of the Poem

It seems that the lines forming the acrostic משה בן אש (lines 23-29)
do not belong to the V i n e   poem, i.e., to the first 22 lines and the
final line, even though they are copied as a direct continuation in one
manuscript. We here briefly present the proofs:

4.3.1.   The word הגפן (vine), which is the main motif of the poem and
           appears in nearly all its lines, does not appear in even one of
these additional lines.

4.3.2.   All seven extra lines are about one subject, which is, however,
           not stated explicitly. Placed where they are as a continuation
to the poem they should refer to the last subject mentioned (in line 22),
i.e., the Elders of Bathyra. Lines 27-30, however, refer to the ages of
the Macabees (אפפוס צרות ממלכי יונים) and it is impossible that the subject
is the Elders of Bathyra.

4.3.3.   Just as the additional lines do not fit the poem from the point
           of view of content, so too do they not fit from a stylistic
point of view. The poem is metaphorical, nearly every line containing some
imagery, whereas in the additional lines there are no metaphors and the
style is narrative.

4.3.4.   The addition of the superscription in MSL seems just as
           artificial as the combination of the two poems. In the

superscription the "roots of the vine" are the Patriarchs - in the poem
itself the "roots" are Joab, Abishai and Asahel (line 21) while the
Patriarchs are the "branches" (line 7); in the superscription the "young
twigs" (יונקות) of the vine are the sages - in the poem there are no
"young twigs" while the "sages" of the vine are "Moses and Aaron and
Miriam, their sister". (line 8).

4.4. Moses Ben Asher

As stated above,[310] nothing is known about the source on which the
homily of the V i n e poem (lines 1-22, 30) was based and thus about
its author. However, we tend to believe that the author of the seven
additional lines was indeed Moses Ben Asher; not only on the basis of the
acrostic, of which the last letter is missing, but also because of the
similarity of the language used in those lines to that in Moses Ben
Asher's colophon to MSC:[311]

... והעצימו והגדילו המק' עשרים וארבעה ספרים   ו י י ס ד ו ם

ב א מ ו נ ת ם   ב ט ע מ י   ש כ ל   ב פ י ר ו ש   ד י ב ו ר   בחיך מתוק

ביופי מאמר ...

and in our poem:

שעשועים ,(line 26)   ב א מ ו נ ת ם   י ס ד ו   פ ר ו ש   מ ק ר א

ה ת ק י נ ו   ט ע מ י   מ ק ר א   ב ש ו ם   ש כ ל   ו נ י ב   מ פ ׁ ר ש

.(line 24)

4.5. A Rabbanite Author

Whether this assumption is correct or not, there can be no doubt that
the author of the seven additional lines was a Rabbanite:

4.5.1. The reference in line 27: "Their souls they have given for the
Tora of our God to make the many righteous (להצדיק ר[ב]ים), to
extend the Tora" is certainly to Israel's self-sacrifice in the Hasmonean
period, when "Afflictions surrounded them from the kings of the Greeks"
(line 28). Can the poet possibly be accused of intending to hint at a
"Karaite term," מצדיקי הרבים, in these lines? According to the Karaite
tradition which ante-dates the secession to biblical times, the Karaites
have no part in the historical event described. The term "to make the
many righteous" as used here merely means to teach Tora to the many and
thus extend it (cf. Isaiah 42:21) just as the מצדיקי הרבים of the
superscription means teachers in exactly the way the term is interpreted
in the Talmud:[312] "'and they that turn many to righteousness (ומצדיקי
הרבים)as the stars for ever and ever' (Daniel 12:3) this refers to the
teachers of children (אלו מלמדי תנוקות)".

4.5.2. The poet accepts R. ᶜAqiva's view that סיג (מסורת or מסורות)
לתורה and states: "They have erected as a fence (סיג = גדר)
round the Tora of our God well-arranged Masoras to instruct the ignorant"
(line 25). The poet is also aware of the rabbinic homily to ושום שכל[313]
and uses it: "As delights they have established the accents of Scripture
(טעמי מקרא), giving sense (בשום שכל) and distinct utterance" (line 24).

4.5.3. Above all, the last lines (27 - 29) of the section leave no
doubt: "Their souls they have given for the Tora of our God to
make the many righteous, to extend the Tora. Afflictions surrounded them
from the Kings of the Greeks and they exiled them and dispersed them to
No (Egypt) and its provinces. The holy tribes rose up against them and
d e d i c a t e d   l i g h t s   (c a n d l e s) on their fall."

There is no doubt that the revolt of the Macabees is being described
here. The Greek kings who pressed them were exiled and scattered[314] to

"No and its provinces"[315] after the holy tribes rose up (or "made war"[316]) against them, and they "d e d i c a t e d   l i g h t s
(c a n d l e s) on their fall", i.e., of the Greek kings. Can there be a clearer reference to the festival of Ḥanukka? a   f e s t i v a l
w h i c h   t h e   K a r a i t e s   d o   n o t   r e c o g n i z e ?
These lines are incontrovertible evidence that their author was a Rabbanite and not a Karaite.

4.6. Conclusion

We have demonstrated, therefore, not only that no proof can be deduced from the Vine poem that Moses Ben Asher was a Karaite, but that, to the contrary, there is every indication, particularly from the lines which bear his name in the acrostic, that he was a Rabbanite.

5. AN AFTERMATH OF THE CONTROVERSY

5.0.   This study was first published in two parts in *Sinai* vol. 20
תשי״ז (August (No. 5) and September (No. 6) 1957). A short time
afterwards Prof. Moshe Zucker published, in the first number of *Tarbiẓ*
27 תשי״ח (October, 1957), a paper in Hebrew entitled "Against Whom Did
Seʿadya Gaʾon Write the Polemical Poem *Essa Meshali*?" in which he reached
the same conclusion as I had, i.e., that Ben Asher was not a Karaite.

It is interesting and somewhat amazing that we both had taken up a
problem that had not been discussed for years and that, although from
different disciplines, we reached the identical conclusion practically
simultaneously. The methods of proof were also nearly identical which
itself strengthens the conclusion reached.

5.1.   In both articles the following (according to Zucker's order)
points were identical: The interpretations given to מוקש in DQHT[317] and to
the expression הוריה כתורה[from the Prophets] ומורים מהם[318]; the position
of Ben Asher regarding the origin of the vocalization and accentuation[319];
the refutation of the proofs Klar brought from sections that have no
connection with Ben Asher[320]; the whole treatment of the Vine Poem - both
the refutation of the proofs that Klar deduced from it and the clear
indications that its author was a Rabbanite, including the decisive proof
in the mention of the Ḥanukka lights[321]; the presentation of the positive
attitude of the Rabbanites to the masoretes, including Ben Asher[322]; and
the reliance on further Rabbanite indications in DQHT both in the language
and terminology and in the content.[323]

The similarity in method is surprising particularly in the way the arguments for Ben Asher's Karaism were rejected and even more so in the specific details and in the sources cited. Naturally the articles do not duplicate each other and the structure is different but the conclusion reached by both is identical - Ben Asher was definitely not a Karaite.

5.2.0.   To the question which this conclusion raises: Against whom did
          Saadia write *Essa Meshali*? we suggested, each in his own way,
different answers.

5.2.1.0.   Zucker believes that this poem was written against the founder of Karaism, Anan ben David, and in order to maintain this opinion he had to neutralize two clear indications which are specifically connected with the name Ben Asher; which he did offhandedly in a footnote.[324] The first evidence is the superscription to *Essa Meshali* in one ms.:   אלרד עלי בן
אשאר עבראני (above 3.0.). According to Zucker this is a mistake or perhaps even a graphic error, and in place of אשאר (בן=)ו   in the original, עאנאן should be read. The other indication, the testimony of Dunash in his responsa to Saadia that "he (i.e. Saadia) responded to Ben Asher" (above 1.1.0.2.; 3.0.), does not, in Zucker's opinion, refer to a specific composition against Ben Asher but rather to a responsum to him in one of Saadia's works.

5.2.1.1.   I am doubtful if those two indications can so be made away with. It is perhaps reasonable to doubt a superscription found in one ms., but it is completely impossible to ignore the other piece of evidence, particularly in view of the fact that Klar has shown that the citation in Dunash's statement about Ben Asher is indeed from *Essa Meshali*.[325] This weighty evidence from Dunash is hardly neutralized by the various parallels that Zucker finds[326] between some of the stanzas of Saadia's *Essa Meshali* and ideas and interpretations in Anan's *Sefer Ha-Mizwot*, ideas and interpretations which are certainly to be found, to some extent, in other Karaite works as well.

5.2.2.0.   Zucker, at the time he wrote his paper, did not know of my suggested identification of Samuel ben Asher ben Mansūr as the Karaite against whom *Essa Meshali* was directed. However, even afterwards, he rejected this solution and gave his reasons in his *Rav Saadya Gaon's Translation of the Torah.*[327]

5.2.2.1.   His rejection is based on chronological considerations. He believes that Sahl ben Mazliah, in whose letter (above 3.2.1.) Abū al-Ṭayyib al-Jabalī (=Samuel ben Asher) is mentioned as being among those who disputed with Saadia, is of a later time and is not to be dated before the 11th century (this is, I believe, Zucker's intention). Thus Al-Hītī's testimony should be taken literally, and accordingly Samuel ben Asher was a contemporary of Abū al-Faraj Hārūn, i.e., in the first half of the 11th century. If so, it is impossible that Saadia, who lived in the first half of the 10th century, wrote against him.

5.2.3.1.   This objection is thus based, on the one hand, on the belief that Sahl ben Mazliah is to be dated later (see immediately below) and, on the other, on the reliability of the chronological evidence of Ibn al-Hītī, who lived in the 15th century, i.e., about 500 years after the persons under discussion. I am extremely doubtful whether this is acceptable, and indeed whether this is any less problematic than ignoring Dunash's testimony (5.2.1.1.).

5.2.3.2.   Even according to Zucker, however, the above is unacceptable. Although I established Al-Jabalī's dates independently (see above 3.2.2.2) yet still Zucker claims that I relied on Poznanski and that Poznanski is wrong. Zucker writes: "Dotan relies on Poznanski's opinion (Poznanski 1908, p. 16) who fixes an earlier time for our Ben Asher, for had he lived in the 11th century it is doubtful whether Sahl ben Maẓliaḥ would have known him. Poznanski, however, followed the view that the Rabbanite, Jacob ben Samuel, with whom Sahl ben Maẓliah corresponded, was the pupil of Saadia Gaon and that therefore it is impossible to date Sahl as late as the 11th century (*loc. cit.* p. 31). That opinion has already been disproved by Mann, *Karaitica* (1935a), p. 25 ff."

From Zucker it appears as though Mann rejects the idea that it is impossible to date Sahl as late as the 11th century; i.e., that Sahl was in fact of the 11th century. However, this does not follow from Mann. Mann does reject the view that Jacob ben Samuel, against whom Sahl wrote his letter, was a pupil of Saadia Gaon (and anyway Mann does not date him as late as the 11th century),[328] but as far as Sahl ben Maẓliah is concerned Mann, too, accepts the generally held view that he lived in the second half of the 10th century.[329]

It follows, therefore, that there is no view which dates Sahl ben Maẓliah as late as the 11th century, and there is, therefore, no reason to so date Abū al-Ṭayyib al-Jabalī. Zucker's objection to my suggestion thus disappears.

5.3.   Notwithstanding all this, it is clear that the problem of the identity of the person against whom Saadia wrote *Essa Meshali* is not relevant to the main subject under discussion here. Whether he wrote it as a response against Anan - which does not appear to me to be correct - or whether he wrote it against Samuel ben Asher, known as Abū al-Ṭayyib al-Jabalī, one point has been proven by both Zucker and myself absolutely and beyond any doubt whatsoever and that is that Aaron Ben Asher and his father, Moses, were not Karaites.

5.4.   Although this opinion was adopted by some scholars - as, for instance, I. Ben-Zvi 1960, p. 6 - it has apparently not been easy for some others to abandon a view which was accepted for so many years and, here and there, one still finds expressed the opinion that Ben Asher was a Karaite, completely ignoring both articles or without at least disputing the proofs put forward in them. In only some of the cases is it possible to attribute this peculiar state of affairs to the fact that both articles were written in Hebrew.[330]

Kahle,[331] somewhat lengthily, restates the old argument. He mainly relies on others who formulated the claims for him. Most of them do not apply to Ben Asher directly but rather to the points of similarity between the Karaites and the Qumran sect; the little that does so apply is not new and is based primarily on the use of allegedly Karaite terminology (e.g., אבלי ציון ,אילי הצדק etc.) from which, as we have demonstrated,[332] nothing can be deduced. It is clear that Kahle did not know the two articles on the subject; the fact that they are in Hebrew may be the cause.[333]

It is to be hoped that with this publication in English such shortcomings will be prevented in the future.

N O T E S

1. Pinsker 1860, p. לב; italics in citation are mine.

2. See also Pinsker 1860, p. 163.

3. Schorr 1861, p. 67.

4. Graetz 1895, p. 479-480. For his other proofs see below.

5. Colophon on p. 479a. Graetz cited according to Pinner's *Prospectus* (Odessa, 1845) p. 86.

6. Schröter 1866, p. 21, para. 72.

7. Graetz, although he does not say so explicitly, apparently relied on S.D. Luzatto (1847, 11b), who vocalized the words in question: תֵּלַף תֶּלֶף הָאוֹתוֹת and interpreted it: "it would be fitting for you to learn the letters before writing what you wrote". Eppenstein (1913, p. 72, note 1) still maintained this interpretation although he does not accept the conclusion Graetz based on it.

8. Graetz 1871, p. 9.

9. Graetz 1871, p. 57-58.

10. Hadassi, section 163, letter ל, p. 60b;   בן אשר רײ״ת המדקדק במסורות מכתבך; in section 173, letter נ, p. 70a he refers to him with נ״ע.

11. Gottlober 1865, p. 125, accompanying the translation of the citation of Graetz; Harkavy in his note to *Divre Yeme Yisrael* (hebrew translation of Graetz 1895), part 3 (1893), p. 488, note 183.

12. Regarding this occupation see Eppenstein 1913, p. 43-45; Mann 1920, p. 270; Assaf 1955, p. 114 and others.

13. See above in Graetz's argument. He is even doubtful as to whether MSL was written by a Karaite scribe for a Karaite (see Graetz 1871, p. 58).

14. This is the famous Bible Codex (*Keter*) from Aleppo; these expressions are from the long colophon which was at its end. See below 1.3. on this ms.

15. Compare the expression ראש המדברים at the beginning of *Sefer Moznayim* of A. Ibn Ezra (Offenbach 1891, p. 2a).

16. Lipschütz 1935, p. ג.

17. In *ᶜAdat Devorim* of Joseph ha-Qosṭandini (Harkavy, *Hadashim gam Yeshanim*, part I, book 2, p. 12) the Hebrew translation runs: החלוף אשר נתחלפו בו שני המלמדים.

18. Levy 1936, p. י.

19. According to Mann 1922, p. 48, all the Masoretes listed there - and not only the Ben Ashers - were Rabbanites.

20. With regard to earlier periods an example is Samuel bar Shilat who was a teacher of young children and who made many statements concerning the laws of writing a Tora scroll and Mezuza (e.g. T.J. Megilla 1:11); another example is the midrash to Song of Songs 1:17: "'The beams of our houses are cedars' refers to the scribes, 'our panels are cypresses' refers to the children" (Yalquṭ Shimᶜoni 985), and many others.

21. Saadia's commentary to *Sefer Yeẓira* 2:2. (Ed. Lambert, Arabic section, p. 45).

22. Graetz 1895, p. 480, note 1.

23. Baer-Strack 1879, p. XXXVIII (Ms. F88, Public Library, Leningrad).

24. Strack, *Alexander Kohut Memorial Volume* (1897), p. 572 (Paper-Ms. Tshufutkale, no. 1, in above mentioned library).

25. Baer-Strack 1879, § 19.

26. Mann 1922, p. 119.

27. Mann 1922, p. 279.

28. Assaf 1946, p. 30. Compare Simeon bar Isaac's *qerova* אותותיך for the 7th day of Passover: מלמדי ומשכילי וסופרי (end of section תמך במעגלותיו). See also below, note 100, for a citation from Qirqisānī where the term מורים merely means מלמדים.

29. The correct reading is תְּלֹה אֶלֶף הָאֹותֶת which means "Equip yourself with your weapons, O future historian." See Allony 1949, p. 180; 1951, p. 144 ff., particularly pp. 158-159 and bibliography there.

30. *Die Massora* in Winter and Wünsche's *Die Jüdische Literatur*, part 2 (1894), p. 11.

31. See Skoss 1936, introduction, pp. XXXVI - L.

32. See further on this below (Ch. 3.).

33. See Gottlober 1865, p. 124, accompanying the translation of Graetz.

34. Hadassi, section 173, letter צ, p. 70b.

35. Firkovitch (in Gottlober 1865, p. 124) comments that Hadassi differentiates between Karaite and Rabbanite scholars by using the first person possessive suffix for the former, e.g. משכילי, and the second person possessive suffix for the latter, e.g. יהודה חיוג ויונה בן גאנח ואבן עזרא ז"ל ושאר בעלי הלשון מדקדקיך (Hadassi, section 167, letter ש, p. 63b). However, Firkovitch was careless, for his proof, according to Gottlober, really indicates the opposite, since Hadassi refers to Ben Asher as המדקדק במסורות מכתבך (see above

note 10), i.e. with the 2nd person suffix, which would indicate
that Ben Asher was a Rabbanite.

36. Saphir 1866, p. 191.

37. Graetz 1895, p. 479-480.

38. Graetz is quoting according to Dukes 1846, p. 36-37. However,
since that edition is exceedingly rare we have cited the paragraphs
according to Baer-Strack 1879. We know today that not all which is
included in these two editions really belongs to Ben Asher's DQHT
(e.g. 1.2.0.3.); see DQHT ed. Dotan 1967.

39. Fürst 1862, p. 113-115.

40. T.B. Ḥagiga 10b; Baba Kama 2b.

41. According to Graetz (*Ibid.*) the Rabbanites naively accepted from
the Karaites the term אשלמתא as an alternative name for the
Prophets (אשלמתא קדמיתא = the Early Prophets and אשלמתא בתריתא = the
Later Prophets) not realizing that they were thus deviating from
talmudic conception.

42. For these, and cognate terms - העתקה, סבל הירושה which are the
Karaite chain of transmission from father to son - see Ankori 1955,
p. 10-11.

43. In order to deduce this from DQHT Graetz had to emend the text and
add some words. See below 1.2.2.

44. Graetz 1881, p. 366 note 1.

45. Baer-Strack 1879, §1. Graetz used the version of the Rabbinic
Bible   (Venice 1518),and Dukes 1846, p. 2.

46. Baer-Strack 1879, §3. Graetz cites according to Dukes 1846,
p. 36-37.

47. See Gottlober 1865, p. 126-127, accompanying Graetz's translation.

48. H.M. Pineles, *Ha-Maggid* (1860) No. 40, p. 163, took note of this - although a year later he changed his opinion and accepted Graetz's view that Ben Asher was a Karaite.

49. See Zunz 1865, p. 641-642; E. Ben Yehuda, A Complete Dictionary of Ancient and Modern Hebrew, S.V. שלם (Vol. 15, p. 7182-7183). Others have interpreted שילום - Prophets, by allusion to *haftara* which was called אשלמתא (Klar 1954, p. 308, note 198).

50. Saphir 1866, 16b; 1874, 187-189.

51. Thus the version of MSC (p. 583) which Saphir saw.

52. Except the *ḥalifin* (method of acquisition) of Boaz; however there it is stated that "this was the custom in former time in Israel" (Ruth 4:7) implying that this law was ancient. See Saphir 1874, p. 189, and see Rashi to T.B. Ḥullin 137a, s.v. אנן דברי בריבי שומעין: "The Torah of Moses is called 'Torah' because it was given for all generations; that of the Prophets is only called קבלה (tradition) ..."

53. The Hebrew version דנין דברי תורה מדברי תורה ואין דנין דברי תורה מדברי קבלה (T.B. Nidda 23a) is even more indicative of this. See Poznanski 1902, p. 179 note 2.

54. But only from prophetic statements couched in the form of a command; e.g. that the uncircumcised is unfit for Temple service (Ezekiel 44:9: "No alien, uncircumcised in heart and uncircumcised in flesh shall enter into My sanctuary"); that the knife for slaughter must be examined (I Samuel 14:34: "and slay them here (בָּזֶה lit. with this)"); deeds need witnesses' signature (Jeremiah 32:44: "Men shall ... subscribe the deeds and seal them, and call witnesses") and many more.

55. See the comprehensive survey in Federbusch 1937, p. 69-70.

56. Oppenheim 1875, p. 84. He did not penetrate the matter as deeply
    as Saphir.

57. Oppenheim was not precise in this citation; on p. 84 he cites בה
    and on p. 81, בו. The only versions known to me from the mss. are
    ממנו and מתם (see Dotan 1967, p. 109, 171); however this is
    irrelevant to our matter.

58. Wieder 1957, pp. 165-175.

59. See Gottlober 1865, p. 126-127 accompanying the translation of
    Graetz.

60. Fürst 1862, p. 115 and p. 179 note 407.

61. Dukes 1846, p. 36-37. This version is identical with ms. ר in
    Dotan 1967, p. 92-95 and it is close to the printed version of the
    Rabbinic Bible (מקראות גדולות) Venice 1518, and to that of
    Baer-Strack 1879, §3.

62. According to what was printed by Saphir 1874, p. 187. I compared
    it to a photostat of MSC (p. 583).

63. וכל repeated in ms.

64. Ms. ר has correctly וסתומים, and so has the Rabbinic Bible (cf.
    note 61).

65. Rabbinic Bible: ובמיני' (= ובמינים).

66. On this explanation of the three levels of sanctity see Saphir 1874,
    p. 189, and Oppenheim 1875, p. 90, who cites parallels for this
    comparison of the Bible to the Sanctuary from the homily of Psalms
    73:17 in T.B. Baba Meziᶜa 86a and from Profiat Duran's *Maase Efod*
    p. 11 (Oppenheim's attempt to explain the MSC version as refering

to upper and lower vocalization is unsuccessful). Also see Baer's
comment, Baer-Strack 1879, p. 2, para. h. With regard to the
connection between דביר (sanctuary) and ספר (book) compare Judges
1:11: "the name of Debir before time was Kiriath-sepher" and the
various rabbinic similies on it. See also Ben-Zvi 1957, p. 366.

67. E.g., ובמיניהם (line 8) which sould read ובמינים or ובמנין. Even
the words וכן העליונים והתחתונים (line 7) may be a scribal
repetition from line 4. And there may be other hidden corruptions.

68. I.e., the happenings, renewals (המתחדשים) of each day; the whole
description is allusive to "what is above, what is below, what was
beforetime and what is hereafter". Another possible explanation
is along the lines of a generality and two details: the creation is
the generality and the upper and lower worlds the details; the
future is the generality, going on its own ancient way (nature) and
renewing (unnatural) are the details.

69. I do not understand the exact meaning here, the general idea is
course, behavior.

70. Not only internally disconnected but also disconnected from the
preceeding section by the removal of the expression וכל זה, i.e.
all that has been said until now, an expression which connects the
section to what preceeded.

71. For a detailed clarification and full comparison of all the versions
see Dotan 1967, p. 170-175.

72. As far as I know this word has not yet been adequately explained.
It seems to me that it means masoretic notes written outside the
body of the text, in the margin, see Dotan 1967, p. 168.

73. On "crooked" letters see S. Baer's *Tiqqun ha-Sofer we-ha-Qoré* (2nd

ed. Roedelheim, 1875) appendix p. 18 ff. What he calls הפוכות "inverted letters" are also to be included in "crooked". See also Dotan 1967, p. 173.

74. That the intention here is understanding and interpreting the text is also indicated by the words בעניגו ובמשפטו which in some manuscripts follow the word והבטוי. See also below (2.2.) on the Karaite attitude which is entirely different.

75. Graetz 1895, p. 480. Fürst 1862, note 407 (p. 179) copied Graetz's emended version without comment as though it were the original version in the *Quntres ha-Masoret.*

76. Actually Graetz's emendation is of no value even to him for the emended sentence הכתוב והבטוי והמוקש דומה לכתב הקודש does not make sense: "The written text ... resembles (!)   the Holy Writ"!

77. Baer-Strack 1879, p. 2, commentary note e: *Das mit der heil. Schrift Verknüpfte, Zusammenhangende,* or possibly according to Bacher 1895c, p. 300: Compared to the Holy text, i.e., that which does not belong to it but is only compared to it.

78. Thus in all manuscripts except MSA for our knowledge of which we must rely on Baer in the variant reading of Baer-Strack 1879. However Baer misled the reader in that he inserted the word והקדש into the body of the text of DQHT on the basis of this manuscript which apparently contained a reading similar to that of MSC, i.e., a pre-edited version in which the word והקדש was in place.

79. On this see Poznanski 1902, p. 179 ff.; also Klar 1954, p. 303-308.

80. See also Eppenstein 1913, p. 51, note 4.

81. Klar 1954, p. 309.

82. *Kuzari* 3:49 (ed. Hirschfeld, p. 198); Judah ibn Tibbon translated

the term אנשי הסברא ("the men of reason" *ibid.* p. 199). They are also known by the term המתקוששים, e.g., in the Commentary to the Decalogue of Nissi ben Noah (Pinsker 1860, p. 9 *et al.*).

83. Hadassi (section 169 letter ב, p. 64b.) does, however, mention one scholar who does not accept the principle of analogy, namely Joseph ben Noah who apparently lived at the beginning of the 11th century (see Skoss 1928, p. 9).

84. Graetz transcribed דעת twice in place of דעה.

85. *"Die Analogie oder die Erkenntnis"*.

86. Some Karaites list 4 hermeneutic principles, e.g., Sahl ben Mazliaḥ (2nd half of 10th century) and even Judah Hadassi (section 168 letter ב, p. 64b).

87. See Klar 1954, p. 307-308.

88. See Abraham ibn Ezra quoted below 2.1.

89. Klar 1954, p. 309 note 205.

90. His Commentary to the Decalogue (Pinsker 1860, p. 11).

91. Klar 1954 (p. 308, note 196) copied the printing error, אפונה, from Graetz 1895, p. 444 and artificially interpreted it as מפוקפקת (doubtful).

92. Compare a similar phrase in Elazar Ha-Kallir's *piyyut,silluq* for the first day of Shavuᶜot אלה העדות והחוקים.

93. Perhaps the phrase קלה וחמורה does not indicate the accepted distinction between severe and light c o m m a n d m e n t s but rather that of the talmudic statement (T.B. Erubin 21b): "New and old, which I have laid up for thee, O my beloved (Song of Songs 7:14) - these are the light commandments and these are the

severe commandments ... these are from the Tora and these are from
the scribes" (הללו מדברי תורה ... אלו מצות קלות ואלו מצות חמורות
והללו מדברי סופרים) And likewise in T.J. Sanhedrin 11:6 30a:
"R. Ishmael stated: The words of the Tora... have leniencies and
severities but the words of the scribes are all severities"
(דברי תורה...יש בהן קולים ויש בהן חומרין אבל דברי סופרי' כולן חומר).
This would be in the sense of the detail immediately following:
מצוות קלות are the words of Tora (דעה and ציווי) and מצוות חמורות
are the words of scribes (עדה).

94. Compare T.B. Megilla 19b: "'And on them was written according to
all the words, which the Lord spoke with you in the mount'
(Deuteronomy 9:10) - this teaches that God showed Moses...what the
scribes were going to reveal (i.e. legislate) in the future."

95. Particular attention should be paid to the phrase ויפה ברורה which
is a good explanation of the rational commandments, i.e., they are
self explanatory (e.g. "Thou shalt not kill") and intelligence
would require their observance even if they were not written in the
Tora (see Saadia's *Emunot we-De'ot*, section 3).

96. See this use of ציווי as arbitrary commandment in Saadia's *Essa
Meshali* p. 525: "צִוְּגָיו לֹא יִכְתֹּב לָנוּ שָׁרְשָׁם" (He did not write for us
the reason for His ציוויים).

97. After Daniel 12:3, 10.

98. A great number of examples are brought by Gottlober 1865,
p. 125-126 accompanying Graetz's translation; Baer-Strack 1879,
introduction p. XIII - XIV; Rosin 1881, p. 517 cites (according to
note 1 p. 66, in his *R. Samuel b. Meir als Schrifterklärer*)
examples from the *mahberet* of Menahem ben Saruk. Further examples
are to be found (ed. Filipowski) on pp. 4a, 15b, 16b, 33a, 33b

et al. See also Ben Yehuda's dictionary, S.V. משכיל (vol. 7, p. 3431.)

99. Cited by Harkavy as in note 11 above.

100. Nemoy 1939 (section 1, end of chapter 3) p. 31:

وهم ... يزعمون انهم ناقلة وانهم أخذوا عن النبوة وانهم اصحاب اللغة
وانهم هم الـ משכילים والـ מורים .

which means: "and they (the Rabbanites) ... claim that they have the tradition and that they received the transmission from the prophecy (prophets) and that they are the masters of the language and that it is they who are the wise (המשכילים) and the teachers." The word מורים (teachers) is the parallel of מלמדים which has been discussed above (1.1.1.).

101. *Essa Meshali* p. 519, lines 18-19 (if the emendation there is correct).

102. Rosenthal 1948, p. נא (שה verses, line 7). See also citation above (note 28) from the *qerova* of Simeon bar Isaac.

103. Mann 1920, p. 49 note 2; p. 141 note 1. With regard to אבלי ציון (Avele Zion) see also Assaf 1955, p. 91.

104. A further proof of Klar will be discussed in the next chapter in the discussion of DQHT's attitude to vocalization (2.3.1.1.).

105. Originally as printed in the Rabbinic Bible (Venice, 1518) and in *Quntres ha-Masoret* (Dukes 1846) and later in Baer-Strack 1879.

106. See Dukes 1846, intro. p. 4 and Baer-Strack 1879, intro. p. XIV - XVII.

107. Klar 1954, p. 308-309, attempted to find indication of Karaism also in §65 of Baer-Strack 1879. However this chapter is one of interpretation and summation (perhaps really Karaite) to the

preceding chapter (§64) *"Interpretation of Ketiv wela Qere"* and is not to be found in the manuscripts of DQHT; furthermore its "question and answer" style is foreign to DQHT's author. It certainly does not belong to the work as do not the chapter *"Interpretation of Ketiv wela Qere"* and the preceding chapter. Here it is not, however, the right place to treat this question in detail. Klar accepted the view of Lipschütz (1935, p. 8 note 1), who attributes to Ben Asher only the versified sections in DQHT, and stated (Klar 1954, p. 291 note 89) that he, Klar, quotes Ben Asher accordingly in his article; it is therefore amazing that he here relies on this section which is not versified at all.

108. Graetz 1871, p. 55-56.

109. MSC, colophon on p. 586. The colophons of MSC were published in Kahle 1959, p. 92-96 and plates 7-8; Kahle 1961, plates 11-17.

110. MSC, colophons on p. 582, 583.

111. Graetz repeats this idea in Graetz 1881, p. 366 note 1.

112. MSC, colophon on p. 583. The actual text in manuscript reads המועדים על ראות; Graetz copied from Saphir 1866, 15a, but the word המועדות is his emendation.

113. MSC, colophon on p. 586.

114. Graetz 1871, p. 57.

115. Gottheil (1905, p. 639; and see also Saphir 1866, p. 14a) who saw the actual manuscript testifies that it is not complete at the beginning. Others assumed from this that the manuscript originally comprised other books of the Bible, perhaps even a complete Bible. However, in the photograph the first pages of the Book of Joshua seem to be intact and there are no pages previous to it. Kahle

(1954, p. 166) is also of the opinion that MSC comprised originally
only the Prophets.

116. MSC, colophon on p. 583; thus also in colophon on p. 582:
" .... זה הדפתר הנביאים שהקדיש"۔

117. MSC, colophon on p. 585.

118. Its meaning here is the same as מחברת or קונטרס (see T.J. Peʾa 2:6,
17a and T.J. Ḥagiga 1:8, 76d).

119. It is difficult to accept the view that rejects the veracity of
Moses Ben Asher's colophon on external evidence. S.Y.Ḥ. Soqer's
point (*Beth Mikra*, 2nd year (1957) p. 5 (ג)) that the Radbaz
(R. David ben Zimra) does not mention MSC, is no proof, since MSC
was, in his times, in Karaite hands. The suggestion to date the
colophon later also raises paleographic difficulties. Teicher
(1950, p. 17-25) also attempted to undermine the reliability of
the attribution of MSC to Moses Ben Asher; his assumptions are,
however, riddled through with inexactitudes and his main proofs
are refuted below in this study and notes. However, the
abundance of the ga^cya and the *meteg* signs in MSC and the ways
of vocalizing which are foreign to Ben Asher do arouse doubts as
to the "purity" of the pointed text, and already Yalon (1955,
p. 261) commented that "the connection of MSC to Ben Asher is
tenuous" referring to Aaron Ben Asher's pointing; but there is no
doubt, to my mind, about the colophon. See however what I wrote
regarding MSC's pointing, Dotan 1967, p. 70-71.

120. T.J. Shabbat 1:1, 2d.

121. T.B. Baba Batra 157b.

122. Graetz, however, did not see the ms. and relies on the

transcription in Saphir 1866, 14b-15a. Saphir, however, explicitly
distinguishes between "the actual hand of the scribes and his ink"
and "another script".

123. Graetz 1881, p. 366 note 1.

124. Colophon on p. 586 which is in Moses Ben Asher's hand.

125. Colophon on p. 585 which is also in Moses Ben Asher's hand.

126. Colophon on p. 588 which is in an entirely different hand. Graetz
took out here the words יעבץ בן שלמה(after the word הקדיש),which
became superfluous after they have already appeared in h i s
(i.e. Graetz's) colophon.

127. Colophon on p. 583 which is also in a later hand and squeezed
into the margin. It should be pointed out that Graetz in no way
indicated his act of "collation" here. Graetz's tendency to doctor
quotations to fit his own ends is known. See G. Deitsch in his
essay תקופת מאה שנה, היינריך גרץ (Heinrich Graetz, a Century),
printed at the end of A. Schmerler's חיי גרץ (The Life of Graetz)
(N.Y., 1921) p. 134-135.

128. The word זכה here undoubtedly means "purchased, acquired" (see
dictionaries) which is also the meaning of the continuation:
ועשה אותו לעצמו להגות בו מעמלו ומיגיע כפיו ומזיעת אפו (and not
as translated by Kahle 1959, p. 92). Compare also the language
of the colophon at the beginning of MSL:

זה המחזור מקרא שלם נכתב ונגמר בנקודות ובמוסרות ומוגה יפה ... מה
ש ז כ ה   מבורך בן יוסף בן נתנאל הידוע בן וזדאד הכהן   ו ע ש ה
א ו ת ו   ל ע צ מ ו   להגות בו מעמלו ומיגיע כפיו ומיזיעת אפו ...
In this case we know (from the colophon at the end) that the scribe
of this ms. was Samuel ben Jacob and that Mevorakh ben Joseph

certainly did not write the ms. but only bought it. - For this
meaning of עשה ל- "purchase" see *Targum Onqelos* and *Pseudo
Jonathan* to Genesis 31:1 and Deuteronomy 8:17; and Rashi and Ibn
Ezra to Genesis 12:5. Also compare among the Elephantine papyri
in the famous letter of Bagohi, the governor of Judah (A. Cowley,
Aramaic Papyri of the Fifth Century B.C., p.112; papyrus #30 line 13)
ולנפשהום עבדו in however a slightly different sense (the semantic
proximity of עשה/עבד is like that of לקח = take to לקח = purchase).
See also S. Abramson, *Leshonenu* 21 (1957), p. 99-100.

129. This is clear from the sentences ולא יוציאו אותו מ ב י ת ו
וכל מי אשר יוציא אותו מ ח צ ר   י ע ב ץ (colophon on p. 588) and
ש ל מ ה ב ן (colophon on p. 582) *et al*. Another indication is
the fact that Jabez ben Solomon is not mentioned in the colophons
with the eulogistic formula. It may perhaps mean a synagogue on
Jabez's name which was called חצר יעבץ בן שלמה "the courtyard of
Jabez ben Solomon" and the word מביתו may mean the permanent site
of the codex.

130. At the time of the purchase; that is, if the term הבבלי in the
colophon on p. 585 also refers to Jabez and not only to his father.

131. In all periods: see Saphir 1874, p. 186; Assaf 1936, p. 230
(particularly note 138); Ben-Zvi 1957, p. 368.

132. MSC, colophon on p. 586.

133. A form of 1st person singular.

134. = כמו שהבינו (as they understood).

135. E.g., אילי הצדק, the opening of the *seder* in Simeon bar Isaac's
qerova, אותותיך, for the 7th day of Passover (edit. A.M.
Habermann, 1938, p. 69).

136. Klar's reliance (1954, p. 314) on Japhet ben ʿAlī's description of the Karaite scholars as אילי הצדק is amazing. The expression, אבלי ציון, which Japhet uses to describe Karaites is also from the quoted verse in Isaiah and is also borrowed from the Rabbanites. See above note 103.

137. MSA also returned to Rabbanite ownership after it had passed into Karaite hands. Kahle (1927, p. 7-12) reconstructed the chain of events slightly differently since he dated the superscription קודש לה' על ישראל הרבנים... to the first half of the 11th century and did not take into account Graetz's correct assumption in this matter (see above 1.3.0.2.4.).

138. The first of them was W. Wickes (טעמי כ"א ספרים *A Treatise on the Accentuation of the twenty-one so-called Prose Books of the Old Testament*, Oxford 1887 [Reprint: 1970, Ktav Publishing House, New York], p. VII-IX); A.E. Harkavy (*Ḥadashim gam Yeshanim* part I, book 6, p. 7-8) dates the whole ms. later by two hundred years, and he was one of the few scholars who actually saw the complete ms.

139. See Dotan 1965.

140. The version is according to Harkavy (*Ibid*. p. 7) who claims that he examined the colophon "in great detail four times." I do not accept Kahle's (1927, p. 3-5) synthetic version which he created according to   others' publications without having himself seen the actual ms.

141. Which he returned to again in his paper (Graetz 1881, p. 366 note 1).

142. It is amazing that Graetz paid no attention to this fact; neither he nor any of the other supporters of the view that Ben Asher was a Karaite raised it as an argument.

143. Not, however, completely. In the second and fourth chapters some
relatively new arguments will be discussed.

144. I.e., closed and open sections and the scribal layout of the "songs"
in the Tora.

145. Among them Schorr, Gottlober, Saphir, Strack, Bacher in sources
cited in notes above. Also the anonymous דב"יב as cited below,
note 150.

146. Graetz 1871, p. 58.

147. See note 48 above.

148. In Pineles 1861 (p. 268-269) he ignores what he himself had written
against Graetz a year previously on "שילום התורה".

149. He signed himself דב"יב; his real identity is not known to me.

150. The long controversy between Pineles and דב"יב on this marginal
question and what follows from it is irrelevant to our discussion.
The sources are *Ha-Maggid* (1860-1862) and Pineles 1861.

151. See Maimonides, *Yad ha-Ḥazaqa*, *ᵓIssuré Biᵓa* 11:15: "This is not a
valid custom but rather a mistake in those responsa and it is the
way of heretics in those places; they learned it from the צדוקים"
(צדוקים in Maimonides' generation were none other than Karaites).

Also Maimonides' responsa in *Sefer Peᵓer ha-Dor* (Amsterdam,
1765): "And they followed the heretical custom (מנהג מינות) to the
extent that they wash themselves in drawn water (a well known
Karaite custom - A.D.) and think that they are thus purified from
their menstrual flow and are permitted to their husbands. This is
nothing but absolute heresy and something which God did not command"
(responsum no. 152, 31b.). Furthermore in Maimonides' responsa to
the Baghdadian Joseph ben Gabir in A. Ashkenazi, *Taᶜam Zeqenim*

(Frankfort a/Main, 1854): "But with regard to the Egyptian Jews we
have found that they deviate towards heresy (דברי מינות) and follow
the Karaite prayer book" (p. 74) and later "And the ban (mentioned
loc.cit. in *Pe'er ha-Dor* - A.D.) shall apply: cursed be any woman
who shall not count (after her menstrual flow) seven clean days or
who shall not immerse herself or shall only wash herself as the
Karaites do". From these responsa, incidentally, it is clear that
no distinction is to be made in Maimonides between the terms מין
and קראי. See also Abraham ibn Ezra (commentary to Exodus 20:23)
who calls the Karaite Ben Zita (Zuta) by the appelation מין.

152. See Mann, JQR, NS XI (1920-1921) p. 470.

153. See the indices of Wilensky's edition of *Sefer ha-Riqma*.

154. See *Sefer ha-Shorashim*, s.v. דרך, דרבן *et. al.*; *'Eṭ Sofer* (Lueck,
1864) p. לא; commentary to Judges 6:19, Ezekiel 16:18 *et. al.*; and
in many places in *Mikhlol*.

155. Regarding another work see Dotan 1967, p. 20.

156. Rosenthal 1948, p. לז line 6; Allony 1959, p. י. Scheiber 1956
(p. 291-303) published a further fragment and deduced from it that
the author was attacking the masoretes. Relying on the accepted
view that *Essa Meshali* was written against the masorete Aaron ben
Asher, Scheiber even went so far as to say that the author of
Ancient Questions was attacking Ben Asher! However, in this further
fragment there is no attack whatsoever against masoretes. I hope
to treat this matter elsewhere.

157. See *Essa Meshali* p. 509 lines 29-36, where he stresses that only the
Rabbanites understand masoretical matters.

158. Ms. F88 in the Leningrad public library; published in Baer-Strack

1879, p. XXXVIII-XXXIX, also in Mann 1922, p. 48-49. Mann, however, erred and transcribed at the beginning of the fragment (which is not cited here) בעלי לשון המקרא in place of המקרא (!) בעלי בעלי.
The change might have been made deliberately; he, however, makes no mention of it.- The whole section has the character of a provocative question and not one asked for information; the enquirer sees Ben Asher as an authority and provokes the Karaites by asking them to explain Ben Asher's vocalization. This is not according to Klar (1954, p. 294) who considers the question to be an objection to Ben Asher's authority.

159. This (ובן) is the correct reading instead of the printed וכן. -This sentence, from וכן to מין, is corrupted in some printed editions and I have used the text in the Schocken Pentateuch, 1937.

160. "The sages of the Tradition", the traditionalists, אלנאקלין (= the transmitters) in the words of Judah Halevy, *Kuzari*, section 3, 49 (p. 198 in the Hirschfeld edition).

161. For the thought contained in the last sentence see above 1.2.3.

162. He calls them אלאגביא (= fools, ignoramuses). See *Kitāb Jāmiᶜ al-Alfaẓ*, Skoss 1936, p. 254 line 148.

163. Such as *Ḥilluq* (p. 106) and, later, Ibn al-Hītī (Margoliouth 1897), and after him Mordecai ben Nisan, the author of *Dod Mordecai* (Vienna 1830, p. 11b) and Simḥa ben Moses ha-Luzki, the author of *Oraḥ Ẓaddiqim* (Vienna 1830, 21a/b) and others. Even Hadassi in *Eshkol ha-Kofer* does not give Ben Asher the appellation משכיל as he usually does to Karaite sages.

164. The Karaites, as is known, are accustomed to recite the memorial prayer for all their departed sages from the times of Anan, after

the completion of the synagogue service every Sabbath. See the
Karaite prayer book סדר תפלות הקראים (Vienna 1854), part 1
p. 303-306.

165. See Baer-Strack 1879, introduction p. X, note.

166. *Dod Mordecai*, p. 15b.

167. It seems that the author of *Ḥilluq* was not later than the 12th
century (see Poznanski 1908, p. 72), however, his identity is by
no means clear; see Gottlober 1865, p. 158 in note.

168. See Schorr 1861, p. 67; Gottlober 1865, p. 143.

169. Pineles 1861, p. 276-277; A. Firkovitch's note in Gottlober *Ibid*.

170. *Ḥilluq*, p. 102-103.

171. Read: רְאוּ (imperative).

172. It should read: במשרת (= with a conjunctive accent).

173. The Karaite method in their polemics is well known: they do not see
their own deficiencies and attribute them to their adversaries.
Their internal differences of opinion are also known not only in
biblical interpretation but even in basic questions of the practical
observance of the commandments.

174. This is posed as a question.

175. In the imperative.

176. Qirqisānī, Nemoy 1939 (section 2, chapter 17) p. 138-140. The
Hebrew translation of the piece in Klar 1943, p. 34-36.

177. He uses the same metaphor elsewhere, *Ḥilluq* p. 101, where he mocks
the Rabbanites for the differences of opinion in the Mishna and
Talmud.

178. Unless the copyists - including Pinsker - changed it.

179. On the traditions of the vocalization of the word יששכר, see Yalon
     1955, p. 258 note 7.

180. It would be worthwhile examining whether there was not, at the time
     of the author of the *Ḥilluq*, a tendency in Karaite works to record
     the *qere* everywhere and ignore the *ketiv*, in order to avoid
     doubling the biblical text. There are many mss. which do this
     occasionally; see, e.g. in C.D. Ginsburg's edition of the Bible the
     two words which the author of the *Ḥilluq* quotes; and see also the
     testimony of Qirqisānī, regarding the system of ʾIsmaʿīl al-ʿUkbarī
     who does not take the *qere* into consideration at all and only reads
     the *ketiv* everywhere. Nemoy 1939, section 1, chapter 15, p. 56:

     אן אסמעיל אלעכברי אבטל אלכתיב ואלקרי וזעם אן אלקראה יג'ב אן תכון

     עלי מא הו מכתוב   See also section 2, beginning of chapter 23
     (*ibid.*, p. 161).

181. Hadassi, section 173, letters ס and ע, p. 70a and likewise
     elsewhere.

182. Klar 1954, p. 290-291.

183. One cannot rely on an expression such as תלמידי תורה and establish
     it as Karaite (Klar 1954, *ibid.* note 79) just because Sahl ben
     Maẕliaḥ uses it as an appellation for Karaites in one of his
     letters of rebuke (Pinsker 1860, p. 33), and that not as an
     independent title but as a metaphorical doublet of the usual
     appellation בני מקרא (or בעלי מקרא). The term תלמידי תורה here
     merely means "students of the Tora" - not even the most naïve
     Karaite would suggest that vocalization was given to Karaites
     exclusively "so that they should not err in reading (Scripture)".

184. Klar 1954, p. 298.

185. Whatever its real meaning is, דקדוק certainly was not given from Sinai.

186. There too Klar (1954, p. 298-299) deduces that vocalization was given from Sinai from the sentence (§3): כלם שבים לסדור הזה בבית קדש הקדשים והקדש וחצר אהל מועד which means, according to Klar, that the script, vocalization and accentuation are not the invention of the Scribes but that they originate (שבים - lit. return) from the סידור (= ספר תורה, i.e., the divine Tora) which was in the Temple. However, according to this interpretation what does הסדור ה ז ה mean? And why קדש הקדשים והקדש וחצר אוהל מועד? Was the סידור in all three? Furthermore, where does Ben Asher state that "all sections of the Bible are equal in value" (Klar 1954, note 147). Klar's interpretation does not fit the version of MSC, and see above 1.2.2. on this.

187. MSC, p. 586. See above 1.3.1.3.

188. Similar to Moses Ben Asher's statement in his colophon (see above 1.3.1.3.) that the "congregation of Prophets" established the biblical books with "accents of understanding".

189. Rosenthal 1948, p. נא.

190. Assaf 1946, p. 15. This is definitely not a Karaite expression, in spite of Wieder 1962, p. 90-91.

191. See above, 2.3.1.1.

192. This is exactly what *Dod Mordecai* (p. 15a) argues.

193. A.Z. Rabinowitz in his translation to Bacher 1895a (*Nizzané ha-Diqduq*, translator's note on p. 59) suggests this trait is connected with the historical concept of the Karaites according to which the future is more important than the past; the imperative

being considered one of the *modi* of the future tense. This theory
is however untenable since, in their paradigms the Karaites do treat
the imperative and the future separately; and the future comes after
the past. See note 194.

194. E.g., in Skoss 1936, s.v. בט (p. 212), s.v. עשה (p. 413) and many
others. Even when he cites the verb form to illustrate other matters (e.g. the conjunctive *waw*) he cites it in the order of:
imperative, past, future - צֵא וְיָצָא וִיֵצֵא ...;רְאֵה וְרָאָה וְיִרְאֶה;עָשָׂה וְעָשָׂה וְיַעֲשֶׂה
(p. 2) with a complete differentiation between imperative and
future.

195. E.g., in the fragment published by S. Munk, *Notice sur Abou'l-
Walid*, p. 21, and see Munk's note there. Also in the appendix to
his commentary on Hosea, Japheth ben ʿAlī brings explanations for
various difficult grammatical forms, and in his explanation of the
conjugation of the verb form he always uses the imperative as the
basic form. This appendix was published (with a German translation) by R. Schroeter in the *Archiv* of Merx, vol. II (1871),
p. 25-29, according to a ms. in the Bodleian Library, Oxford.
Later Hirschfeld (1926, p. 103-105) published it according to a
ms. in the British Museum.

196. See Bacher 1895b, p. 242 note 3.

197. E.g., in his commentary to Genesis 6:3 (Skoss 1928, p. 129).

198. *Zikhron La-Rishonim*, part 1, book 5, p. 74 ff.

199. According to Bacher (1895a, p. 50 note 5; p. 55 note 3) this
section is by a Karaite.

200. = present tense.

201. הזמן העתיד includes the imperative; see above, note 193.

202. See our reservations on this above 1.2.5. and 2.3.0.

203. E.g., on p. 89 to the words מקללים להם (I Sam. 3:13) and on p. 580
to the words קֹבְעים אֹתִי (Malachi 3:8) *et. al.*

204. See Saphir 1866, 17a and various sources quoted in Baer-Strack 1879
p. 44 for §57.

205. Graetz 1871, p. 56, note 1.

206. פִי אִיצִ׳יאח פסאד דעואהם. This is the title of chapter 22 (of section
2) which deals with this matter. See Nemoy 1939, p. 153-161.

207. The *Masora magna* to Numbers 1:1 (Rabbinic Bible).

208. See Saphir 1866, 16b-17a; Oppenheim 1870, p. 365 and particularly
Oppenheim 1875, p. 79-90; Bacher 1895c, p. 293-304.

209. On the question of ideas from the *Sefer Yezira* in DQHT see Rosin
1881, p. 521; Bacher 1895a, p. 24.- Graetz (1871, p. 58 note 1)
argued that *Sefer Yezira* is religiously neutral (his term is
confessionslos); it is however known that the Karaites denigrated
and ridiculed any interest in Kabbala or mysticism. See Eppenstein
1913, p. 51. And see also Salmon ben Jeruhim's sharp attack on the
mystical literature of the Rabbanites such as the *Sefer Razim,
Sefer Shem ben Noah, Otiyyot de-Rabbi ʿAqiva, Shiʿur Qoma* (Davidson
1934, chapter 14, p. 111, 113 and notes there). Even Qirqisānī
attacked this literature (Nemoy 1939, section 1, chaps. 3 and 4,
p. 15, 31. On other books see editor's index, vol. 5, p. 042-043).

210. This is close to the rule יש אם למסורת (see Ovadiah Bertinoro's
commentary to the Mishna). The idea is hinted at elsewhere in DQHT
(see above 1.2.2.) and we have already seen the *Hilluq's* opposition
to it (above 2.2.).

211. See above 1.2.3., and also the citation above 2.1. from Abraham ibn

Ezra: "Each person interprets the verses according to his whim...
also in the matter of the commandments and laws...they are
continually changing from side to side according to their state of
mind".

212. MSC, p. 584.

213. This ending is identical with *Seder ʿOlam Rabba*, 30 (ed. Rattner,
     Wilna 1897, p. 140).

214. MSC, p. 586.

215. See Saphir 1866, 16b.

216. Klar 1954, p. 276-281.

217. See above 1.1.2. This is on the assumption that both the
     superscription to *Essa Meshali* and Dunash's statement refer to
     the same composition. For a summation of the pros and cons to this
     assumption see Allony 1951, p. 146.

218. It has since become clear that these "alleged indications" are in
     sections which do not belong to DQHT and are not to be connected
     with Aaron Ben Asher. See above 2.3.0.

219. And it is major, consisting of more than 500 stanzas of between
     3 and 5 lines each. The material which has come to light up till
     now is about one third of the entire composition; it has been
     published by Lewin (1943, p. 505-532).

220. In addition to a general attack on the Karaites, Saadia goes into
     great detail with regard to Karaite law such as: *ẓiẓit, mezuza,*
     phylacteries, grace after meals, style of prayers, calendric
     reckoning, consanguineous marriage, levirate marriage, menstrual
     women, etc.

221. Pineles 1861, p. 276 writes: "For they (Ben Asher and Ben Naftali -

A.D.) were not aggressive Karaites who engaged in polemics against the Rabbanites but rather masoretic grammarians who faithfully followed their craft."

222. Lewin 1943, p. 497.

223. Lewin 1943, p. 504 supplies a detailed table of this plan.

224. At least in what has up till now reached us of *Essa Meshali*.

225. Only eight of the hundreds of lines in the hitherto discovered fragments deal with Masora.

226. Lewin 1943, p. 517, lines 7-8. Saadia proceeds to describe the purity and ethical qualities of the Talmudic sages.

227. See Lewin 1943, p. 509, lines 29-36. He does not invalidate such interest but only denies Karaite competence.

228. One of the first mistakes was in the interpretation of the word האותות in Dunash's citation from Saadia, which they understood, according to Luzzato 1847(11b), as referring to letters. They therefore saw it as a response to Ben Asher, the grammarian. This is not so; for the correct interpretation see above, note 29.

229. See Lewin 1943, p. 494; Klar 1954, p. 288.

230. The colophons are no indication of his being well known.

231. Pinsker 1860, p. 37, from which Mann (1935a, p. 25 note 46) copied. It was first printed by M. Steinschneider, *Catalogus Codicum Hebraeorum Bibliothecae Academiae Lugduno-Batavae* (1858), p. 403. In the following notes we shall present the variant readings in Steinschneider's edition.

232. עתה

233. This word is lacking.

113

234. בעלי

235. מבקשים

236. עמהם

237. במלחמות

238. Add: בנינו

239. ומנה

240. לבלתי צאת

241. ולא

242. ירוחם. For the name form see Davidson 1934, p. 1 note 1.

243. This word is lacking - which is the more correct version; see Mann 1932, p. 382 and bibliography cited there.

244. אשא

245. משלי

246. Should read: ואחוד

247. Add: יצ"ו

248. עליהן

249. כמסמרים

250. אלנבלי - which is a mistake.

251. וגם

252. כיסון - which is a mistake.

253. חוטן

254. Steinschneider suggests: אמתת

255. Literally: let out from under his hand.

256. Certainly Steinschneider's reading אשא משלי ואחוד is the correct one, and it has since been discovered in a Geniza fragment.

257. Pinsker 1860, p. 64. Poznanski (1908, p. 17) questions this genealogy because of the doubt as to the reliability of the introduction (מקדמא). However, this doubt is with regard to the introduction of Salmon ben Jeruḥim, whereas this genealogy is in the introduction of Levi ha-Levi ben Japheth, which nobody except Poznanski (1904a, p. 49 - without giving any reason) has questioned. Pinsker (1860, p. קיא), Fürst (1865, p. 46), Gottlober (1865, p. 207), Steinschneider (1902, p. 85, §46) and others all accept this genealogy. The dates which Poznanski (1908, *loc. cit.*) fixed for ʿAlī ben Ḥasan are most amazing if we compare them with those he fixed for his son (*Ibid.* p. 20).

258. Margoliouth 1897, p. 429-443.

259. *ibid.*, p. 435.

260. Margoliouth's emendation; ms. has אבר.

261. Ms.: ותנאצ'רא; the substitution of צ'/ט' in mss. is a well known phenomenon.

262. Thus Margoliouth's emendation; ms. has ורדה.

263. See Bacher 1895b, p. 253.

264. Klar (1954, p. 288, note 60) rejects, by this argument, the possibility that Saadia wrote against Al-Jabalī.

265. It seems that Salmon's answer to *Essa Meshali* was written during Saadia's lifetime, for otherwise it would have been sufficient for Sahl to list him once only in the consecutive list of the posthumous answers. See Davidson 1934, p. 2.

266. According to other uncorroborated Karaite testimony Salmon was older than Saadia and was his teacher (see Davidson 1934, p. 1; Lewin 1943, p. 501). Ibn al-Hītī (Margoliouth 1897,p. 434) even goes so far as to report that Saadia participated in Salmon's funeral and mourned him bitterly. This is an obvious exaggeration.

267. See above 3.2.1. and note 257.

268. Ben Mashiah lived in Baghdad (see Ibn al-Hītī, Margoliouth 1897, p. 434). However, Abū ʿAlī Hasan al-Basrī, i.e., Japheth ben ʿAlī, lived most of his life in Jerusalem; the appellation al-Basrī indicates his family origin (see Birnbaum 1942, p. VII). His father, ʿAlī ben Hasan, who is also listed by Sahl, may have lived in Basra.

269. Salmon ben Jeruhim apparently lived in Aleppo. According to Ibn al-Hītī (Margoliouth 1897, p. 434) he died there.

270. According to Mann (1935a, p. 25, note 46), Al-Jabalī originated from Jibāl, i.e., Media. But see Pinsker 1860, p. 37, note 1; Fürst 1865, p. 48, note 159; Poznanski 1904b, p. 16.

271. Thus in the letter under discussion to Jacob ben Samuel he says: "I have come from the Temple (בית המקדש)" (Pinsker 1860, p. 27 and 30) which means Jerusalem (cf. Arabic בית אלמקדס = אלקדס). See Assaf 1946, p. 40, note 53 for many examples of this usage of בית המקדש.

272. See Poznanski (loc. cit.) and 1908, p. 17. See also Steinschneider 1902, p. 79, §42. Fürst (1865, p. 48), however, antedates him to 935.

273. Harkavy published the Hebrew opening verses to these questions in Ha-Goren 1 (1897), p. 91.

274. Poznanski (1904b) also stresses this.

275. Margoliouth 1897, p. 442, note 8.

276. Menahem was not necessarily alive at that time; c.f. discussion
     above 3.2.2.1. regarding Saadia's responsa against Anan.

277. There is, however, another possibility that has not yet been
     suggested. Assaf (1933, p. 35-53, 193-206) published *The Polemic
     of an Ancient Karaite against the Rabbanites* and estimated that it
     was part of a composition of Ibn Sāqawayh written as a response to
     Saadia Gaon's composition *Kitāb al-Radd ʿala Ibn Sāqawayh*. Davidson
     (1934, p. 27) agreed that Ibn Sāqawayh was the author, but felt that
     it was a response to another of Saadia's works *Kitāb al-Radd ʿala
     al-Mutahāmil*. Mann (1935b, p. 67, note 199) questioned the
     attribution of authorship to Ibn Sāqawayh. It should be pointed out
     that there are several allusions in *Essa Meshali* which seem to be
     direct refutations to one of the points made by that ancient
     Karaite. The Karaite wrote: "Tell us about your early ones such as
     Shammai and Hillel, ʿAqavya, ʿAqiva, Dosa, Joshua and the other
     disciples about whom your predecessors - and you - have admitted
     that they did not serve their teachers enough and that thus
     conflict (between them) increased." (English translated from
     Assaf, *Ibid*. p. 194). In *Essa Meshali* we find (p. 510): "Your
     monstrousness closed your ear, your wickedness has carried you
     away and you have lifted your eyes on high against Hillel and
     ʿAqiva"; and later: "You have done stupidly...you have rebelled
     for you have provoked God's sages"; and later (p. 517): "He
     destroys his own soul in his anger, while insulting God's sages,
     and stretches forth his hand against them... he w r o t e   that
     they misled the Jews deceitfully acquiring financial gain...", and
     he goes on to enumerate the good qualities of the talmudic sages,
     amongst them those whom the ancient Karaite accused of not having

"served sufficiently". Is it possible that there is a connection between these two compositions? Could it be that Abū al-Ṭayyib al-Jabalī is that ancient Karaite and that Saadia wrote *Essa Meshali* as a reply to that attack? It will be difficult to answer these questions until more material is discovered about al-Jabalī, but this possibility should be considered.

278. C.f. 3.2.1.

279. At the end of this chapter in which we have touched on *Essa Meshali* it is fitting that we express our reservations about the date of that work which was fixed by Klar (1954, p. 314 ff.) to be between 915-921. These dates were fixed for two reasons: a) since *Essa Meshali* was written against Aaron Ben Asher who lived in Tiberias it is reasonable that Saadia wrote it when he lived in Palestine and Tiberias, i.e., in the suggested years; b) Dunash, in his responsa to Saadia, cites from him a verse: ברקת וזהב ויהלם, וראמות וכדכד ואחלום, חבורת צדק הקדושה (Schröter 1866, p. 23 para. 87) in order to disagree with the form אחלום which Saadia created for prosodic rhyming purposes instead of אחלמה. Klar estimates that this verse belonged to the שֶׁת group in *Essa Meshali* and relying on this estimation assumed that the whole composition could not have been written later than 921, which is the year of the great calendric controversy between Saadia and the Palestinian Ben Meʾir; for after that year, in the heat of the controversy, it is inconceivable that Saadia would have used such an appellation of honor as חבורת צדק הקדושה to describe the Palestinian Sanhedrin at whose head the rebellious Ben Meʾir then stood.

The first reason is of course untenable according to our theory. With regard to the second, if the assumed origin of the verse in question is correct then it would appear that Saadia did write it

before 921, but it is reasonable to assume that he wrote it in
Babylon near to Jibāl, the residence of Samuel ben Asher. It is
known that Saadia left Egypt for a period before he went to
Palestine in 915 and during that period he spent some time in Syria
and Babylonia (see Malter 1921, p. 425; Simḥoni 1924, p. 497). It
is therefore possible that he composed the work in his youth near to
the year 905, in Babylonia or afterwards on his return from there to
Egypt. His famous *Kitāb al-Radd ʿala ʿAnan* was, after all, written
in 905, which shows that he had already then started his anti-
Karaite activity.

280.   Klar 1954, p. 310-311. Kahle 1959, p. 83-86, has since published
       the poem again, but with some errors, adding also an English
       translation.

281.   I have examined photographic copies of the three mss., namely, MSL,
       that in the British Museum (=BM) and that in Cambridge (=C). A
       photocopy of the latter was published by Kahle 1959, plate 9. For
       a description of these mss. see Klar 1954, note 209. The more
       important variant readings brought below in notes (deviations of
       plene and defective spelling are ignored) are from my reading of the
       mss. I do not believe that C and BM belong to one ms. (as Klar *loc.*
       *cit.*note 209 suggested),because in BM the script is slightly
       different; the lines and the script are more cramped; there are
       more lines to the page; and particularly there is a difference in
       writing the Divine Name - in BM it is with two *yods* and in C
       with two *yods* and a *waw* between them.

282.   MSL נטעתה (not as Klar, *ibid.*, note 210).

283.   MSL הגפנים (no ms. reads גפנים).

284.   MSL אֹרֶן definitely so vocalized; the final *nun* is doubtful - it

might be a *zayin* or possibly a small final *nun*,after Isaiah 44:14
אֹרֶן (see Biblia Hebraica[3], viz. MSL, and in some of the variants
in C.D. Ginsburg's Bible edition.Other variants there have a *ketiv*:
zayin and a *qere*: *nun*).

285. MSL היתה

286. MSL זְמֹרוֹת, so vocalized; BM זמירות (*plene*); no reading of זְמֹרֹת.
The word זמיר or זמירה here means branch(not so in dictionaries!).

287. MSL לוּלַבֵּי, so vocalized.

288. MSL סְמַדְרֵי, so vocalized.

289. MSL עַנְבֵי, so vocalized.

290. MSL כִּנְרוֹתֵיהֶם, so vocalized.

291. MSL סָמוּךְ, so vocalized.

292. בתירה see below note 304.

293. C ולהגדיל

294. C in נתעוררו there is an indistinct line under the second *resh* and
it is possible to read the word as נתעורכו.

295. MSL ותמלוך (Pinsker 1860, p. קכא in note, has it wrong).

296. Klar 1954, p. 312-314.

297. See above 2.4. and note 212.

298. There is a wealth of biblical allusion in the poem; cf., the vine
poem in Isaiah 5 and the parables in Ezekiel 17:6-8; 19:10-14; cf.
particularly: Genesis 49:11, Isaiah 5:2 (to line 1); Isaiah 5:7 (to
line 3); Ezekiel 17:8, 19:11 (to line 5); Ezekiel 17:7, Psalms
80:12 (to line 6); Psalms 106:16, Isaiah 61:6 (to line 16); Joel
2:16 (to line 18); Daniel 12:3, Isaiah 42:21 (to line 27) *et. al.*

299. See above 2.3.1.2. According to the most post-dating Karaite

tradition the secession of the Karaites took place in the times of Judah ben Ṭabbai, whereas there are those who ante-date it to Rehoboam the son of Solomon (see *Ḥilluq* p. 100, *Oraḥ Ẓaddiqim* p. 17).

300. Incidentally, the interpretation of the poem is not necessarily so. See below 4.3.2.

301. Even the story as it is in T.B. Rosh Hashana 29b, indicates moderation, and it is entirely impossible to see them as the militant dissidents of the Talmud. There, too, their opinion cannot be considered "minority opinion according to which the law is not decided" since they did not know the law and wanted to discuss it. See Tosefta, Pesaḥim 3:9 (ed. Zuckermandel p. 162).

302. See above, end note 299.

303. See *Dod Mordecai* 10a, which follows Moses ben Elijah Bashyazi's *Matṭé ha-Elohim*.

304. Even the reading בְּתִירָה in MSL is doubtful. It is written with a *waw* between the *taw* and the *resh* and with a somewhat indistinct *ḥolam*, there is also an indistinct *pataḥ* under the *bet* and an indistinct *dagesh* in the *taw*; it would thus read בַּתּוֹרָה (?) (and if so it would merely be a general appellation for the sages, זקְני בַּתּוֹרָה). However, there is a distinct *ḥireq* under the *taw*, a *raphe* sign on it and a sort of short diagonal line through the *waw* (the *ḥireq* and the diagonal line are stronger and more distinct than usual - they may be a later addition?); the reading would thus be בְּתִירָה (perhaps בְּחִירָה?).

305. Above 1.1.1.

306. Above 1.2.4.

307. Above 1.3.1.3.

308. See above 1.2.4. and note 101.

309. See Mann 1917, p. 478, note 22.

310. Above 4.2.1.

311. See above 1.3.1.3. and note 132. Klar noticed this similarity.

312. T.B. Baḇa Batra 8b. in the story of Rav Samuel bar Shilat. See also the commentary attributed to Saadia Gaon on this verse in Daniel.

313. See above 2.3.1.2.

314. נִפְצְגֻם as הפיצום; the occasional פ"נ/ע"יו substitution.

315. The emendation to [לנ]א as the rest of the emendations in square brackets is Klar's. If the emendation is correct the reference is to Egypt (נא = the capital city of Egypt); however, נוא is also an ancient city in Bashan, see I. Press, *A Topographical-Historical Encyclopaedia of Palestine* vol. 3 (Jerusalem 1952), p. 624, s.v. נוה (variant נוא).

316. נתערכו from מערכה, meaning "to make war", and see above note 294.

317. Above, 1.2.2.; Zucker 1958, p. 61-62; Dotan 1957, p. רצ.

318. Above, 1.2.1.; Zucker 1958, p. 63; Dotan 1957, p. רפז.

319. Above, 2.3.1.1-2.; Zucker 1958, p. 63-64; Dotan 1957, p. שח-שו. Zucker, however, does not draw the necessary conclusions from the differences between the various texts of the passage under discussion (see above 1.2.2.). On this matter see also the similarity in detail between Zucker 1958, note 28 and myself, Dotan 1957, end of note 75 (in the present study the end of that note has been deleted; it its place see above note 78).

320. Above, note 107; Zucker 1958, p. 66; Dotan 1957, p. רצה note 104; Zucker even rejects each proof particularly (p. 66-67).

321. Above, 4.; Zucker 1958, 67-70; Dotan 1957, p. שסב-שנז. Even the
     most detailed points are identical, e.g., above, 1.2.4. and note
     101, and 4.2.3.; Zucker 1958, p. 69 and note 48; Dotan 1957, p.
     רצד, שס. Also the suggested emendation בחירה < בתירה above, end of
     note 304; Zucker 1958, p. 69; Dotan 1957, p. שם note 286.

322. Above, 2.1.; Zucker 1958, p. 70-73; Dotan 1957, p. שג-שא. Even
     detailed proofs, e.g., Zucker 1958, p. 72 second paragraph; Dotan
     1957, p. שג.

323. Above, 2.3.1.2. and 2.4.; Zucker 1958, p. 73, 75; Dotan 1957, p.
     שיב-שיא, שט.

324. Zucker 1958, note 80.

325. Klar 1954, p. 281-288.

326. Zucker 1958, p. 75-81.

327. Zucker 1959, p. 143-144, note 584.

328. Mann 1935a, p. 26.

329. Mann 1935a, p. 22.

330. Thus in 1971 when the Jerusalem *Encyclopaedia Judaica* appeared, its
     article "Ben-Asher, Aaron Ben Moses" (Vol. 4, col. 465-467) still
     expressed the old view that Ben Asher was a Karaite. Since this
     article is an adapted translation of the similar article in the
     Encyclopaedia Hebraica (Vol. 9) which appeared back in 1957, it
     repeated all the arguments in favor of Ben Asher's Karaism as
     formulated in the *Hebraica*. These arguments have, however, been
     refuted one by one both by Zucker and by myself. No mention is
     made of this fact. The only "adaptation" made in the English
     version of the *Judaica* is the sheer remark (in brackets) that Dotan
     and Zucker "hold that Aaron Ben-Asher and his family were not
     Karaites". Had this remark not been added one could have considered
     the English article as a mere translation of an obsolete article (as

is the case, e.g., with the Bibliography of this article; it
contains nothing new compared to the original article, not even
Zucker and Dotan). This remark, however, is an attempt to make the
English article appear up-to-date, an attempt that is hardly
successful, since it neglects the new arguments and facts and
simply disregards them. But the impression the reader gets (as did,
e.g., Reiner 1973, p. 24-25), as if the old view about Ben Asher's
Karaism is maintained there on sound proof and solid consideration,
is misleading; there is not one new argument, not one argument that
had not been refuted, and refuted twice by two persons working
independently and from different approaches.

331. Kahle 1959, p. 97-105. He also repeats himself in a later book,
Kahle 1961, p. 65-66, where he even reiterates other scholars'
arguments, p. 69-72; on this see above, 1.2.2. and Dotan 1967,
p. 175-176.

332. See above, 1.2.4., 1.3.1.3., 4.2.3., and Zucker 1958, p. 69,
particularly notes 48 and 49.

333. He does mention (Kahle 1959, p. 105 note 3) Zucker's article once
but does not discuss its content. He apparently did not know of
my article.

BIBLIOGRAPHICAL REFERENCES AND ABBREVIATIONS

Allony, N., 1949

"תלף", לשוננו ט"ז (תשי"ח-תשי"ט); 180-187

_____., 1951

"תִּלּוֹף תֶּלֶף לרסטי"ג", סיני כ"ח (תשי"א); קמד-קסא

_____., 1959

"המלים הבודדות בישאלות עתיקותי", HUCA 30; א-יד

_____., 1964

"סדר הסימנים (חיבור קראי בדקדוק המסורה מתקופת משה בן אשר)",
HUCA 35; א-לה

Ankori, Z., 1955

"Some Aspects of Karaite - Rabbanite Relations in Byzantium on the
Eve of the First Crusade", Part I, *PAAJR* 24; 1-38.

Assaf, S., 1933

"דברי פולמוס של קראי קדמון נגד הרבנים", תרביץ ד' (תרצ"ג); 35-53,
193-206

_____., 1936

"לתולדות הקראים בארצות המזרח", ציון א' (תרצ"ו); 208-251

_____., 1946

Texts and Studies in Jewish History [Hebrew].

_____., 1955

תקופת הגאונים וספרותה

Bacher, W., 1892

Die Hebräische Sprachwissenschaft vom 10. bis zum 16. Jahrhundert.
Mit einem einleitenden Abschnitte über die Massora [= J. Winter und
A. Wünsche, Die Jüdische Litteratur seit Abschluss des Kanons, II.
Band, 119-235].

125

Bacher, W., 1895a

    Die Anfänge der Hebräischen Grammatik [= ZDMG 49].

‗‗‗‗‗‗‗., 1895b

    "Le grammairien anonyme de Jérusalem et son livre," *RÉJ* 30; 232-256.

‗‗‗‗‗‗‗., 1895c

    "Rabbinisches Sprachgut bei Ben Ascher," *ZAW* 15; 293-304.

Baer, S. - Strack, H.L., 1879

    Die Dikduke Ha-T^{e}amim des Ahron ben Moscheh ben Ascher und andere
    alte grammatisch-massoretische Lehrstücke zur Feststellung eines
    richtigen Textes der hebräischen Bibel.

Ben-Zvi, I., 1957

    "'מקדשיה' הירושלמי וכתרי-התורה שבבתי הכנסת הקראיים בקושטא ובמצרים",
    קרית ספר ל"ב (תשי"ז); 366-374.

‗‗‗‗‗‗‗., 1960

    "The Codex of Ben Asher", *Textus* 1; 1-16.

Birnbaum, P., 1942

    The Arabic Commentary of Yephet ben ͨAli the Karaite on the Book of
    Hosea.

Davidson, I., 1934

    The Book of the Wars of the Lord, containing the polemics of the
    Karaite Salmon ben Yeruhim against Saadia Gaon.

Dod Mordecai

    מרדכי בן ניסן, דֹד מרדכי (וויען 1830)

Dotan, A., 1957

    "האמנם היה בן-אשר קראי?", סיני כ' (תשי"ז); רפ-שיב, שנ-שסב

‗‗‗‗‗‗‗., 1965

    "Was the Aleppo Codex Actually Vocalized by Aharon ben Asher"?,
    Tarbiẕ 34, 136-155 [Hebrew].

Dotan, A., 1967

The Diqduqê Hattĕ‛amim of Ahăron ben Mošе ben Ašér with a critical
edition of the original text from new manuscripts [Hebrew].

DQHT

Sefer Diqduqé Haṭṭe‛amim.

Dukes, L., 1846

קונטרס המסורת המיוחס לבן אשר ז"ל

Eppenstein, S., 1913

Beiträge zur Geschichte und Literatur im Geonäischen Zeitalter.

Essa Meshali

תקה-תקלב; Levin 1943.

Federbusch, S., 1937

"גזירה שוה בתור שיטה בלשנית", אזכרה להרב א"י קוק, קובץ תורני-מדעי
ערוך בידי הרב י"ל פישמן, מחלקה ד'; נז-פג.

Fürst, J., 1862

Geschichte des Karäerthums von 900 der gewöhnlichen Zeitrechnung.

_____., 1865

Geschichte des Karäerthums von 900 bis 1575 der gewöhnlichen
Zeitrechnung.

Gottheil, R., 1905

"Some Hebrew manuscripts in Cairo," JQR 17; 609-655.

Gottlober, A.B., 1865

Bikkoreth Łetoldoth Hakkaraim, oder Kritische Untersuchungen über
die Geschichte der Karaer [Hebrew].

Graetz, H., 1871

"Die beiden Ben-Ascher und die Masora," MGWJ 20; 1-12, 49-59.

_____., 1881

"Die Anfänge der Vocalzeichen im Hebräischen," MGWJ 30; 348-367,
395-405.

128

Graetz, H., 1895

   Geschichte der Juden, 5. Band, 3. verbesserte Auflage [I could not
   consult the first edition of this volume which was published in 1860].

Hadassi

   ספר אשכל הכפר ליהודה הדסי בן   אליהו הדסי (גוזלוו 1836)

Harkavy, A.E., 1892

   זכרון לראשונים, חלק א', מחברת ה', חוברת א'

Ḥilluq

   חלוק הקראים והרבנים, Pinsker 1860; 99-106.

Hirschfeld, H., 1926

   Literary History of Hebrew Grammarians and Lexicographers.

Kahle, P., 1927

   Masoreten des Westens, I [Reprint: 1967].

_____., 1954

   "The Ben Ascher Text of the Hebrew Bible," *Donum Natalicum H.S.*
   Nyberg Ablatum; 161-170.

_____., 1959

   The Cairo Geniza, Second edition [First edition: 1947].

_____., 1961

   Der hebräische Bibeltext seit Franz Delitzsch.

Klar, B., 1943

   "ענייני מסורה ומבטא אצל קרקסאני'', ענייני לשון, קונטרס ערוך בידי ח'
   ילון, תש"ג; 31-38] = ב' קלאר, מחקרים ועיונים בלשון בשירה ובספרות
   (תשי"ד), 320-328[.

_____., 1954

   "בן-אשר'', מחקרים ועיונים בלשון בשירה ובספרות (תשי"ד); 276-319
   [= תרביץ י"ד (תש"ג); 156-173, ט"ו (תש"ד); 36-49[.

Levy, K., 1936

   Zur Masoretischen Grammatik, Texte und Untersuchungen.

Lewin, B.M., 1943

"'אשא משלי' לרס"ג", רב סעדיה גאון - קובץ תורני-מדעי בעריכת הרב י"ל

פישמן (תש"ג); תפא-תקלב.

Lipschütz, L., 1935

*Der Bibeltext der tiberischen Masoretenschulen, Ben Ašer - Ben
Naftali, Eine Abhandlung des Mischael ben ⁽Uzziel.*

Luzzatto, S.D., 1847

"עמקי שפה", בית האוצר, לשכה א' (תרי"ז); א-יז

Malter, H., 1921

Saadia Gaon, his Life and Works.

Mann, J., 1917

"The Responsa of the Babylonian Geonim as a Source of Jewish History"
(Part 1), *JQR N.S.* 7; 457-490.

_____., 1920

The Jews in Egypt and in Palestine under the Fāṭimid Caliphs,
Volume I [Reprint: 1970].

_____., 1922

The Jews in Egypt and in Palestine under the Fāṭimid Caliphs,
Volume II [Reprint: 1970].

_____., 1932

"החיבור הפיוטי 'אשא משלי' לרב סעדיה גאון", תרביץ ג' (תרצ"ב); 392-380.

_____., 1935a

Texts and Studies in Jewish History and Literature,
Volume II - Karaitica.

_____., 1935b

"עניינים שונים לחקר תקופת הגאונים", תרביץ ו' (תרצ"ה); 88-66.

Margoliouth, G., 1897

Ibn Al-Hītī's Arabic Chronicle of Karaite Doctors, *JQR* 9; 429-443.

Mishael

Lipschütz 1935; א - כ.

130

MSA

The Aleppo Codex of the Hebrew Bible [only partly preserved; now in Jerusalem].

MSC

The Cairo Codex of the Prophets written by Moshe ben Asher in 895.

MSL

The Leningrad Codex of the Bible No. B 19a in the Saltikov-Shchedrin Public Library.

Nemoy, L., 1939

Kitāb al-Anwār wal-Marāqib, Code of Karaite Law, by Yaʿqūb al-Qirqisānī, Volume I.

Oppenheim, D., 1870

"מאמר לבן אשר", המגיד י"ד, גיליון 46; 365.

_____., 1875

"Ben-Ascher und der angebliche Differenzpunkt in Betreff der Heiligkeit der Bibel zwischen Rabbinismus und Karäismus", *Jüdische Zeitschrift für Wissenschaft und Leben* 11; 79-90.

Orah Zaddiqim

שמחה בן משה הלוצקי, אורח צדיקים (וויען 1830)

[published together with *Dod Mordecai*].

Pineles, H.M., 1861

צי"מ פינילייש, דרכה של תורה

Pinsker, S., 1860

Lickute Kadmoniot. Zur Geschichte des Karaismus und der karäischen Literatur [Hebrew].

Poznański, S., 1902

"Anan et ses écrits," *RÉJ* 44; 161-187.

_____., 1904a

Zur jüdisch-arabischen Litteratur.

Poznański, S., 1904b

"Jabali, Abu al-Ṭayyib al-", *Jewish Encyclopedia*, VII; 16.

_____,. 1908

The Karaite Literary Opponents of Saadia Gaon [= *JQR* 20-28].

Reiner, F.N., 1973

Masoretes and Rabbis: A Comparison of Biblical Interpretations [Thesis
submitted ... for the Degree of Master of Arts..., Hebrew Union
College - Jewish Institute of Religion, Cincinnati, Ohio].

Rosenthal, J., 1948

‏"שאלות עתיקות בתנ"ך"‏, *HUCA* 21; כט-צא

Rosin, D., 1881

Recension [of Baer-Strack 1879], *MGWJ* 30; 515-524.

Saphir, J., 1866

Iben Safir, I [Hebrew].

_____,. 1874

Eben Saphir, II [Hebrew].

Scheiber, A., 1956

"Unknown Leaves from ‏שאלות עתיקות‏", *HUCA* 27; 291-303.

Schorr, J.H., 1861

‏"בקורת ס' לקוטי קדמוניות להחכם ר"ש פינסקר"‏, החלוץ, מחברת ששית
‏(תרכ"ב)‏ ; 56-85.

Schröter, R., 1866

*Kritik des Dunasch ben Labrat über einzelne Stellen aus Saadia's
arabischer Uebersetzung des A.T. und aus dessen grammatischen
Schriften.*

Simḥoni, J.N., 1924

‏"סעדיה גאון"‏, התקופה כ"ב ‏(תרפ"ד)‏ ; 495-500

Skoss, S.L., 1928

*The Arabic Commentary of ʿAli ben Suleimān the Karaite on the Book
of Genesis.*

Skoss, S.L., 1936

The Hebrew - Arabic Dictionary of the Bible known as Kitāb Jāmiᶜ
Al-Alfāẓ (Agrōn) of David ben Abraham Al-Fāsī the Karaite, Volume I.

Steinschneider, M., 1902

Die arabische Literatur der Juden.

Szyszman, S., 1966

"La famille des massorètes karaïtes Ben Asher et le *Codex Alepensis",*
RB 73; 531-551.

Teicher, J.L., 1950

"The Ben Asher Bible Manuscripts," *JJS* 2; 17-25.

Wieder, N., 1957

"'Sanctuary' as a Metaphor for Scripture," *JJS* 8; 165-175.

_____., 1962

The Judean Scrolls and Karaism.

Yalon, H., 1955

"פרשת שלח לך (כ"י ירושלים 2238 .Heb. 8°)", קרית ספר ל' (תשט"ו);
.263-257

Zucker, M., 1958

"Against Whom Did Seᶜadya Gaʾon Write the Polemical Poem *Essa*
Meshali?", *Tarbiẓ* 27; 61-82 [Hebrew].

_____., 1959

Rav Saadya Gaon's Translation of the Torah [Hebrew].

Zunz, L., 1865

Literaturgeschichte der synagogalen Poesie.